Cruising Memories
of the Locked Down Traveller

Bob Kenchington

We acknowledge the Traditional Owners of the land on which we publish books, the Quandamooka people, and pay our respects to Elders past, present and emerging.

Published by Boolarong Biographies
an imprint of Boolarong Press
38/1631 Wynnum Road
Tingalpa Qld 4173
Australia.
www.boolarongpress.com.au

First published 2024

A catalogue record for this book is available from the National Library of Australia

ISBN: 9780975650851 (paperback)

Cover design by Boolarong Press
Typeset by Boolarong Press in Granjon LT Std 12pt

Printed and bound by Watson Ferguson & Company, Tingalpa, Australia

Contents

Prologue

As I write this, the world is in the middle of the, "100 Year Pandemic", Corona-Virus ... and this has nothing to do with drinking too much beer!

Not able to travel for several months now, not even interstate, my wife and I are 'bunkered down' at home with the garden and the garage looking wonderful, with all the maintenance work having been carried out in these areas, over the past few months!

All those items in drawers and boxes, stored in my garage over many years that will, "come in handy one day", have been whittled down, making way for order in the storage sections. Couple this with my new found carpentry skills of making a new work bench, with a support of five drawers under. All this contributing to minimizing the slightly excessive abundance of, "bits" in cardboard boxes of all sizes...and has my wife's full approval!

Being retired, my wife and I have over the past few years, enjoyed travelling. This has included several cruises, on various ships, visiting many regions and cities around the world.

Cruising is certainly not inexpensive however, when the whole experience of travel, bed and board and places visited are reviewed, you undoubtedly realize that through this medium you have often achieved great value for money. Your experiences would also have been completed in style. Something not necessarily achieved by travelling long distances by plane. Indeed, sometimes you have to fly to another country to join your cruise ship and often when your cruise is complete, you have to fly back home. These flights can cost you as much or more than your three-week cruise! And, these flights last only a few hours!

Travelling on a cruise liner can also allow for many days of short-term visits to places, keeping the same bed each night. Also, visiting countries/cities this way for the first time can confirm whether you might want to return to that place for a longer stay in the future, should a destination be special. Alternately of course, you are sometimes pleased that your visit to a certain location was only one day, as you wouldn't want to visit that stop again!

Of course, the shipping line selected and the suite/cabin chosen can vary the cost per day by several dollars. However, our experiences have often been uplifted by, "special deals", "early booking discounts" or "last minute EVERYTHING", being included. And certainly, we have experienced many a good deal by being canny with our bookings.

One cruise we did a couple of years' ago, with the particular suite we had booked even had a special deal included in our room rate, of a free bar on-board and we didn't even know this until we got on board... And yes, we did seem to spend a 'little' more time at this venue!

Travelling via cruising is special and this type of holiday has become increasingly popular over the past few years and the cruise lines and number of ships have expanded considerably in this period.

There are now ships that can accommodate 5000 plus guests, with deck space often given over to large children's play domains. Although this style of cruiser is not for us, the smaller ships with on-board numbers of, preferably less than a couple of thousand, being preferred. Less than one thousand even better!

My wife and I have travelled with a few different cruise lines over the past twenty years, but one ship in particular that has gained more of our custom is the Cunard ship, the Queen Elizabeth. We have completed four cruises on this ship and enjoy the whole experience, indeed our 5th planned cruise on this ship had to be cancelled in recent months due to the Covid-19 virus spreading worldwide.

I must admit that this particular cruise was quite inexpensive, given the extra "bits & pieces" provided and I was very disappointed it was cancelled, but Cunard did the correct thing.

Although we enjoy sailing on the Q.E., it is fair to say that some adjustments could be made to the, very British style of service operation provided and the dress codes sought by the ship's "rules". Although some of these dress codes were relaxed on our most recent trip around Oz and N.Z. (This would probably not occur in Europe though!).

This last trip on this vessel was completed in early January 2020 and only just prior to the pandemic issue being fully recognised.

Prior to this trip it was almost three years since our previous cruise on 'The Queen', which we joined in Feb. '17, leaving from Sydney and concluding in Hong Kong in March 2017.

A four-week cruise in total, covering mostly port cities of Japan and I will come back to this particular journey later in the book.

With that cruise in January 2020 though, we did not know when we commenced this cruise from Melbourne, that this would be our last cruise for some time, due to that Virus and the serious concerns that it has raised in regard to travel anywhere in the future.

Cruise around Southern OZ and N.Z. December 2019 to Jan 2020

This cruise was to commence from Melbourne, so we had flown down from Brisbane and were spending a few days before we embark at our favourite Melbourne hotel, the Park Hyatt in the city.

This hotel has been one of our favourite hotels for over the twenty or so years, since its' conception. This quality hotel was built on vacant land near the St. Patrick's church at the top of town, not far from the Parliament Buildings.

We always feel welcome here with the manager and his team always out and about, talking with guests. The whole team of staff are always friendly and courteous and we feel at home in this environment.

With our planned cruise we will be on board for a journey of three weeks, covering both Southern Australia, Tasmania and then on to New Zealand, having Christmas (and my birthday) and New Year celebrations on board.

The weather at the start of our trip is a little cooler than our home state of Queensland and one reason why we like to move south in the summer months, leaving behind the hot and sticky days in Noosa. Plus, our home town of Noosa is for ever increasing in holiday makers at this time of year and therefore a quieter life is sought!

Well, I must say that departing Melbourne's Station Pier and heading out through Port Phillip Bay in the early evening, attending the ship's usual, "Sail Away Party", is definitely no match for the Sydney experience. Leaving the Harbour dockside opposite the Opera House and sailing past ... The Bridge, well, that experience is ...WOW and worth a million dollars!

Leaving Melbourne's Station Pier, with the view across the bay to the Newport Power Station is just not the same!!

Never mind, we are here to enjoy some relaxing days and stopovers in a couple of great places and about 2000 of our 'shipmates' are doing the same.

Burnie, in Tasmania, is our first port of call... on a Sunday ... Hmmm.

Not exactly a busy, thriving town, but a pleasant little place to stroll around, with a few shops open in the main street, obviously these retailers knowing that a big cruise ship is in port today!

We were in Burnie earlier in the year as part of our two weeks spent holidaying in Tassie in January 2019, once again to escape the Queensland heat and the excess of tourists that lob into our town over this holiday period.

So, we know what to expect from Burnie, a relaxing little town right on the ocean and not much to do but walk along the beachfront this day. One significant joy of doing this particular walk is seeing the Fairy Penguins, that reside in the open rock sections along this section of the beach.

Well worth getting us off the ship for a walk and visiting a little coffee shop in the main street allows us to have a great coffee, (better than on board and at lower prices than the ship!).

Referring back to ship purchases, that is one problem with most of the shipping lines with extra purchases such as drinks, being charged to your account in American Dollars... Quite often over the last few years, our Dollar has been worth an average of 30% less in the exchange rate, so your final on-board account can reflect a little surprise!

Leaving Burnie in the evening we are about to spend the next day at sea, so this day will see us relaxing in our cabin and reading.

We 'acquired' a few magazines along the way with both national newspapers, The Australian and The Financial Review, providing their usual monthly mags just before our trip. Plus, a couple of mags were acquired from the Qantas lounge... as is the norm.

The following day we arrived early into Hobart dock. The weather is good and we're close to the city and all of our usual 'haunts' when in Hobart. Mures Seafood, right on the wharf and with the best Crayfish display, being one highlight.

Across the road, a couple of minutes away, is Salamanca Place and a little further on, the historic sector of Battery point, for a great coffee and freshly baked cake. All of these sectors are all within an easy walk of our berth.

However, this day we have decided to hire a car from Avis and do a little drive around and visit a few outlying suburbs that we don't usually get to.

Picking up the car was not too difficult, with only a ten-minute walk necessary from the ship to their city office.

After collecting our car our first stop was to be Kingston Beach, where we were earlier this year and thought it was very attractive and a suburb where we could spend more time, when on an extended visit in the future.

This time around the place appears a little quieter, not what we remember, the cafes not so full and the beach area also quiet. A short walk is taken along the beachfront and then we got back in our car and headed 5 minutes up the road to Kingston township.

A little cheating here … this penguin sits outside in the small town of Penguin, situated a few klms. along the coast from Burnie.

After a quick stop at the local Coles supermarket, to buy some ladies socks (for my wife, not me), we head off back up to Battery point for a coffee at the famous Jackman and Mc Ross Bakery. We not only have the best coffee we've had for some time, but we indulge in a freshly baked apple and sultana "scroll"... read, bloody big soft and delicious puffy cake! We share and are still full!

Following this stop we head off to Salamanca Place, have a short wander around the shops, decide to buy a lottery ticket (which didn't win) and then we jumped back into the car and headed out of town.

A short drive and we are heading over the bridge and up the motorway towards the airport, but we will be passing this to investigate a little beach cove called Carlton Bay, a little further north.

Hmmm! Carlton Bay is not bristling with shops or cafes, it's just a surf beach and rocks! And I haven't surfed for many a year, so not for us this day.

So, ...lunchtime is fast approaching and, on our drive up to Carlton Bay we passed the Barilla Bay Oyster Farm, not far from the airport and a venue we have eaten at before, so know of its' great fish and Oyster dishes. So, an easy decision for lunch, we head straight there and get the last table available, the restaurant being quite busy.

From the restaurant itself, you have views over the working Barilla Bay oyster farm and further views will take in the unique wetlands and onto Mount Wellington.

A "one plate shared dish" of a dozen oysters Kilpatrick, a piece of crumbed fish, a small piece of salmon and a few Calamari rings and accompanying dipping sauce … oh, and a small bowl of chips is ordered to share and is delicious! Oh, and a light beer as well… I was driving!

Following this it's a slow drive back to the city to drop off the hire car and walk back to the ship, checking out the crayfish display at Mures on the way...

Not to buy, just to drool over, as dinner is on board and we are not self-catering!!

We do love Hobart and Tasmania in general and all it has to offer, especially the food sectors and we will be back soon… well, as soon as travel opens up again!

Our designated dining room on board this cruise is the Queens' Grill, being the 'top' restaurant on board. However, my wife and I, having been on board this ship three times before, know that there will sometimes be … deficiencies.

The menus are obviously designed and written to entice you to select that, mouth-watering selection you love. However, we also know that the written word is very often over inflated and not representative of the end product placed before you by your designated waiter.

Take yesterday's lunch… The menu states: Salt and Pepper Calamari, with a green salad and a sweet Chilli dip!

The actual product served; 2 deep fried squid rings, no salt and pepper evidenced, a few leaves of Rocket lettuce and the dip is just 2 or 3 spots of sauce on the plate …hardly dipping sauce. Mind you, with the very small portion of Calamari you would not need a dipping sauce! And salt and pepper Calamari is usually flat sliced small oblong sections, with a salt and pepper coating. My offering was nothing like this.

Now that was the starter. The main course I chose was 'Croque-Monsieur', a French dish usually of toasted fresh sourdough bread sandwich, with ham and cheese in the middle and cheese covering the top and then grilled or toasted to finish,

My lunch consisted of what I can only describe as a stale white bread sandwich. It contained some sort of 'smear', not cheese on the inside plus ham, at least it resembled ham and nothing on the outside and not toasted!! It was worse than even a ham sandwich … it was disgusting in all senses. Of course, comment was made!

Dinner was better. However, the menu advertised dessert of; Bakewell Tart … this was no Bakewell Tart… Bryan, our waiter delivered a small oblong sponge effort on "custard" and this sponge cake bore no resemblance to a tart at all. I returned it with comment, suggesting the chef should go to a Coles supermarket and buy a packet of Mr. Kipling's Bakewell tarts, so as not to get confused again! Definitely not the best day for the "top restaurant"!

Well, with a day at sea, the next morning we're sailing into the region of Kangaroo Island, off the coast of South Australia. At this planned stopover we are supposed to be taking the ship's Tenders across to the local port, as the ship is too big to dock. However, this morning there is significant wind and it is not safe to use the Tenders. Unfortunately, our Kangaroo Island visit is cancelled.

Now this is the period whereby the bush fire season had commenced and that very afternoon, a very large fire started on Kangaroo Island and this was definitely not the place to be.

So, maybe a good omen not being able to go ashore earlier this day! (That fire developed and in the following few days, the Island was severely damaged.).

I should also make note here, that this period was the start of a very large section of fires spreading across the southern part of the Australian coast.

For the rest of this cruise significant smoke was often affecting the ship's journey, even on the ocean.

Being unable to dock at Kangaroo Island, the ship's Captain decided to move on to our next scheduled stop of Adelaide a day early and stay overnight.

This is a good plan and we enjoyed a day and a half in the "City of Churches". Having been to Adelaide quite a few times over the years we know the city very well and so an enjoyable time was had here, firstly with a trip to the Rundle Mall Shopping precinct, mostly doing window shopping and of course, enjoying the odd coffee and a good lunch.

We also enjoyed a trip across to the large fruit and veg market just off Victoria Square and again, enjoying the wander through the various offerings, including the little coffee and cake outlets… as we do!

Leaving the Port on the second afternoon we had a day at sea and the following morning we arrived back in Melbourne. This destination concluding the ship's, short mini cruise of a few days. This allows new shipmates a chance to enjoy perhaps their first cruise, of a few days, which may encourage a longer trip in the future.

We did a similar trip around Japan …part of our longer, Asian cruise, Cunard obviously endeavouring to drum up business in this sector. The ship completes these in some regions, allowing short trips, which guests can complete, often getting a 'taste' for cruising generally.

So, this day, knowing Melbourne well, having lived there for many years, we took off for a local wander.

As the ship's Shuttle Bus dropped us off close to the Crown Casino Complex, we decided we would have a wander here and a 'window shop' and then have lunch in the Crown precinct… No gambling involved!

Well, lunch was great ... Lucky Chan's Chinese was selected. We miss our Chinese restaurants (Melbourne being noted for its'

Docking in Hobart

Sullivan's Cove, Hobart

selection of quality outlets). We have only one, very poor offering in our home-town…

I think we'll have to move! Melbourne has many excellent Chinese restaurants and Lucky Chan's is certainly one of them.

This day turned out to be a real treat, as when we were walking away from our lunch venue, we went to open a large exit door at the end of the walkway and we bumped straight into two young ladies (although not quite as young now). Jude and Sherrie, who worked for us in our office for a few years, before we sold our business.

It was great to chat and of course hear how their "young families" were now. Twelve years on and they hadn't changed... fantastic.

Leaving Melbourne once more, on Sunday eve we again headed back to Burnie, arriving on Monday morning. Once again for a day, before heading off on our way across, "The Ditch" to New Zealand.

At sea...

Today is Tuesday the 24th December... my birthday... Yes, 28 again!

Returning to our room from our trip to the Buffet for breakfast this morning we are greeted by a display of two bottles of Champagne and seven cans of beer, all displayed on our bed and accompanying this selection is a birthday card from Cunard, signed off by Captain Simon Love and a few of his team.

What a lovely surprise. Now I'm wondering...what will happen in the dining room tonight?

Yes, at dinner the word has gone 'round, to use an expression ... It's Mr. K's birthday. Following the main course and a little delay, the whole team of, Ico the Maitre'd and the other wait staff that serve our table come over to shake hands and wish me Happy Birthday and Voila ... An oblong decorated cake with white icing and Happy Birthday scrolled on top is presented. But, as Ico confirmed... No singing!! What a wonderful end to a perfectly relaxing day.

Christmas Day … well another day at sea and Xmas is everywhere… Other guests with father Xmas hats on, some with other head gear. A Japanese gentleman has golden plastic 'antlers' on his head...all day! Even at dinner he is still with his antlers … and a very posh black Dinner Suit on!

At twelve-noon Father Christmas is still in the Queens Room (the ballroom), presenting presents to kids on board, having had a very large gathering there, commencing from 10.15 am this morning.

Another day at sea and the usual elaborate menus present at lunch and dinner, but as usual, the food on the plate does not always marry with the written word! Ah well, we at least know what to expect having travelled on this ship a few times.

Boxing Day... Yes, it's the day after Christmas... No one seems to want to use the expression, Boxing Day... Not sure why, I must ask.

We awoke this morning to the vast mountainous hills of Milford sound. We are traversing the south waterway of this inland Fjord section of the South Island.

The ship continues to traverse the inland sections of this region, with Doubtful Sound just completed and apparently, Dusky Sound next... Hmmm. It's much like churches and mountains, once you've seen one, you've seen them all!

I have asked the question of a couple of people, one a senior officer; "why is there no reference to Boxing Day", no one seems to know the answer to my question. Ah well, I'll find some other white suit with epaulets on their shoulder and ask the same question...

Dunedin is our stop tomorrow, a town that we have visited a couple of times previously, so a little window shopping is probably as much as we'll do and no doubt grab a coffee. Although one photo we are hoping to get is of a very funny section of road at a main intersection from the main shopping region. When, in a taxi heading back out of town last time we were here, the taxi was situated in the right turn lane, actually two right turn lanes, side by side.

However, as we reached the end of this junction to turn right, painted in the usual white lettering on our section of road, just prior to the right turn arrows, the words shown are; "left turn only"! Duh! ...

Even our taxi driver was laughing and made a statement about the local council being...different!

Well, here we are in that section of Dunedin this day, but my planned photo was not required, it has been changed and the words are now painted out!

So, a cup of coffee and a wander around the shops and we head back to the ship on the next shuttle bus. Interestingly, the Holland America ship, The Nordam is in the same dock as us, at the Port Chalmers, this port services Dunedin.

The Nordam is the ship that we last sailed on in these waters. It's also fair to say that, it is not the best ship we have sailed on, anyway we won't dwell on that. However, I was reminded that when we were in port here on that ship, their shuttle bus service was not free (as is the case with QE and every other ship we have been on). On the Nordam, each way on the bus was a cost of $15 per person ...$30 each way. We caught a taxi as it was half of this cost.

This time, arriving back at the port, I went over and checked out their shuttle service, speaking with one of the ship's staff... Blimey, the same trip into town now is a cost of $20 per person each way! And cash only!! That is rude!

Well, Dunedin was ...OK, but not somewhere that you could say was sensational. However, we had a pleasant couple of hours there and back on board, we are looking forward to our sail away, heading to Akoroa.

We have been to Akoroa a couple of times previously, once by ship and once was via a driving holiday we had in the region some years ago.

This town is reasonably compact and sits on the, Banks Peninsula, with its' rather sparkling sea front. It has a little division of a small harbour, between the two main sections of the town's shops, which also adjoins a small park.

It has a French background as much as an English heritage and this is noted by a couple of French Tricolor flags flying in the town and a couple of major sculptors of French origin in the small park section.

The region, on this small peninsula south of Christchurch, was founded by French Settlers in 1840. It was this French interest in New Zealand that expedited Britain's decision to annex N.Z. and signing the, Treaty of Waitangi, with the local Maori chiefs.

The town also sits in the heart of an ancient volcano area, but no concerns with this in recent times.

If you are lucky, you may see the, "Hector's Dolphins" swimming in this region and having more time available you could join a local tour group (in warmer weather) to spend time in the water having a swim with these wonderful creatures.

Being off the ship early, we decided to partake in a breakfast here, which was good and later after our usual wander around the shops, another coffee was taken, also good. Following this, it was another short review of the harbour and then we ventured back to the ship, via today's Tender service, as no major port facility is available to enable large ships to dock.

Back on deck, it was just the usual relaxing day...of eating ... oh, and that other thing, that usually accompanies eating!

The following day we arrive in New Zealand's capital, Wellington, the world's most southern capital! However, it's Sunday and only a few, mostly major retailers are open.

Again, we have been to Wellington a few times and the shuttle bus, organised by the ship, has two stops this morning. The first being opposite the parliament building, known locally as The Beehive, due to its' circular, tiered design. (Shown below).

Just behind this is the original cathedral, St. Pauls, built in 1866. This is a beautiful Gothic church and well worth visiting. The second bus stop is much closer to the central shopping zone, which is where we alight.

A short walk around this section and we then moved on towards the quite attractive waterfront, with a little window shopping along the way.

We enjoy a good walk for about an hour and then head toward a section of buildings on the waterfront, where we know there are a few restaurants situated, including a couple of very good ones.

Of course, being a Sunday, not only are there possibly more locals out enjoying the day here, but a fair number of our shipmates are also looking for suitable lunch venue.

Being the, 'fastidious foodies' that we are, we check out each restaurant we pass, along this waterfront path, both to see how busy they are (always a good sign of quality product), but also table availability and checking out the food on customer's plates to see the standard.

We eventually decide on, Shed 5 ... An attractive fascia, with dining tables presented with crisp, clean, white table cloths on

them. A very professional young waiter greeted us and we could tell he was not the usual, "backpacker on a limited visa".

We had an excellent lunch of a shared entree of, Whitebait fritters (Whitebait is always excellent in N.Z.) and a little side salad and for main course we both had a Snapper and chips. A simple dish but well executed and delicious, with its' salad accompaniment.

Following this wonderful lunch, we decide to continue our walk back towards the first bus stop, The Beehive, as we are now closer to that pickup point, than our original stop in the city area.

We didn't have long to wait, with a bus pulling up within minutes and away, back to our steel home.

Back on board the ship and we are preparing for another day at sea, before arriving at our final stop, Auckland. Here, we will stay for two days, one overnight and this will be December 31st. Our evening being, New Year's Eve and … Party Time!

My wife and I have visited Auckland many times and have mostly stayed at the very pleasant and relaxing Sofitel Hotel on the Viaduct, with its' friendly and efficient staff. We therefore have a fairly good knowledge of both the city and its' layout and the surrounding suburbs, which again, we have spent time at on our previous stays. On this stopover we even venture over to the Sofitel hotel and wish a couple of the regular staff we know, a Happy New Year!

The reasonably local suburbs of Devonport, Parnell and St.Helliers, being three areas that we always visit and enjoy a coffee or a meal and of course, wandering the shops ... just on the off chance we might find that bargain!

Devonport is always a trip we love, especially via the ferry trip across the harbour and without a car. We get in a reasonable amount of walking here, with a number of diverse shops, including a few with wonderful art works and always worth a look and of course, the eateries!

The two days spent in this region are again good, even with the upheaval of major road works and alterations occurring in the main street, which runs along the port side, disrupting both traffic and pedestrians.

We believe these works were being undertaken by the city to both offer better traffic flow and be a more attractive streetscape, in time for the 2021 America's Cup yacht race, being held in Auckland this time. (The Virus unfortunately placing this on hold).

This day we have decided to do once again, a reasonable 6 Klm. walk to Parnell. However, this day being New Year's Eve, virtually every shop is closed when we get there. We decide to return to the dock area by bus (at $7.00 for 2, a bargain!). The main harbour area is reasonably busy, but a very pleasant lunch at the Botswana Butchery restaurant is taken and is delicious. We have eaten here a few times over the years and never disappointed.

That evening, following a very relaxing dinner in the Queen's Grill, we head back to our suite and being the Eve of the New

Year, we dress a little more informally ready to attend the NYE party on board the ship.

This was a well organised gathering, up on the Lido outdoor section and it was terrific with a huge amount of our shipmates attending this outdoor function. We were all dancing the night away, awaiting the local fireworks display at midnight.

Large platters of 'nibbles' and what seemed like, a huge number of Champagne bottles flowing, were adding to our enjoyment, as it should be!

This New year's entertainment gathering was well organised and Cunard got a big 'tick' for this event, held on-board … PARTY, PARTY and PARTY!!

One of the best New Years' celebrations we've attended and the Auckland Tower Firework display was just superb!

Music was both by a local band, brought on board especially and in between their breaks, our on-board DJ was offering a very

suitable selection of 70's and 80's music, (obviously suiting the generation mostly on board this cruise).

At the strike of midnight, the sky lit up with a massive fireworks display, which appeared to be coming from the Sky Tower up on the city's elevation.

It was magnificent and probably one of the best displays we've seen for some years and a wonderful way to bring in the new year and the new decade… oh was the start of this decade going to be different!

Auckland was our final NZ stop and following the very wonderful party to celebrate the start of the new year, a very 'relaxed' day was planned in the city after the night before. We then prepared for the next 3 days to be spent at sea venturing back to our commencement port of Melbourne.

This cruise, covering Christmas and celebrating New Year and a new decade, was a very enjoyable three weeks and provides many happy memories.

Being a localised cruise, it is of course an easy and relaxed way of spending the Festive Season. And you don't have to worry about any food preparation or… washing-up!

Our Japanese Adventure

Our previous cruise on this ship was an inspiring 28 days and took us mostly to places not visited previously and to different cultures, food and historic overtones and therefore a memory to share.

We arrived early at Sydney Airport, having travelled down from Brisbane in a fast and smooth Qantas A320 Jet. After collecting our three large suitcases from an unusually very slow Qantas carousel, we took a half hour taxi ride to the city. Our very pleasant young taxi driver, whom we chatted to on our journey, telling us he was originally from Afghanistan but now, "I'm an Australian", he happily informs us.

He told us how he had lived in Sydney for thirteen years and that he was only thirty-one with a wife and two sons. He was very pleased to be living in Australia and loved the lifestyle.

I would imagine his lifestyle was very different now, compared to where he was born. His English was excellent and we enjoyed his conversation on our journey into the Harbour City.

In a seemingly shorter time than usual we arrived at the very plush and inviting, Park Hyatt Hotel situated in the famous Rocks area, right on the edge of the more famous Sydney Harbour. We have stayed here a few times over the years. We unloaded our luggage from the taxi and paid our new friend from Afghanistan slightly more than the fare shown and wished him well.

Our delightful hotel has spectacular views across the water to the magnificent Opera House. Unfortunately, our room did not share the same enjoyable views!

Our accommodation for the next two nights was on the 'backside' of the hotel facing the Southern end of the Sydney Harbour Bridge...or more specifically, the very large stone 'anchor point' supporting this section of the bridge.

Being a little more precise, it would have had a view of this section of the Harbour Bridge, except branches from a very large tree right outside our only window blocked most of the view!

Still our room was large and spacious, with a very comfortable king size bed, so big I thought, that the Hulk would have looked small in it and our ensuite bathroom also had heaps of space. AND…to be honest, we were using up some Hyatt Loyalty Points and the room was, … 'free', so no real complaints.

We dropped our bags, the previously mentioned three large cases plus two smaller shoulder bags and ventured back downstairs. We walked past reception and through the casual eating area and out onto the adjacent timber walkway leading across to the, Overseas Cruise Terminal, a short walk away.

We walked over to the Cruise Terminal to assess where we were to head in two days-time, when we were to jump on the Queen Elizabeth (the ship that is, not Her Majesty), which was

CUNARD
14

leaving from this very location. We were joining this section of Her World Cruise, getting off twenty-eight days later in Hong Kong after visiting mostly port cities in Japan and a couple of other Asian outposts, including Shanghai in mainland China and the port city of Busan in South Korea.

After a quick 'recci' of the Cruise Terminal, we decided to walk around the waterfront. Passing the Local Ferry Terminals, we strode across to the immediate shops, leaving the Opera House off our tour, having been there many times before.

Plus, the sky was now turning rather grey and overcast and so we circled back to the hotel, passing along the shops in the main Rocks strip, 'window-shopping' on the way.

We arrived back at the Park-Hyatt and unpacked our clothes for the next two days, leaving the majority content of our suitcases still intact, ready for our next move.

A quick 'phone call was made to confirm a time for our dinner arrangements.

Our first evening in Sydney was already planned, we were having dinner with valued friends, Apollo and Ann-Marie, who we have known for about seventeen years, having first met Apollo (then in Real Estate sales), who was the salesman responsible for selling us our very first home in Noosa.

He and Ann-Marie had re-located from Sydney with their young daughter, their only child at that point, to sunny Noosa, on Queensland's Sunshine Coast.

We became friends and it transpired that they were searching for a new rental house, so we negotiated a deal and they rented that first home from us for a year, which suited both parties at that time. For us, we were getting organized to relocate to Noosa, once our business was sold, but for now, still resident in Melbourne. Apollo and Ann-Marie were extending their time in Noosa, with the recent birth of a new baby boy. They had enjoyed their time in Noosa, but were returning to Sydney at the end of that twelve-month period.

Returning to Sydney at the end of that year, Apollo changed career paths and set up a small catering company and gained a small café contract at a local tennis club in Vaucluse. In this club he was providing the members with both good coffee and a few tips on hitting the ball, him being a big tennis fan. Following a period here he then took on a lease at a council owned Harbour Front venue, growing this business with daily café style service to day trippers and providing the odd function including wedding functions and associated receptions, developing the business to greater heights, through long hours and hard work.

So that first evening in Sydney, Apollo and Ann-Marie picked us up at the hotel and we enjoyed a very relaxed Italian treat at a Bondi Beach Italian eatery. The restaurant was not busy and we virtually had the dining room all to ourselves, providing a laid-back, low-key dinner with good food, good wine and good friends. Afterwards, Apollo drove us back to the hotel, providing a short 'tourist' view of Bondi and surrounds. This was an interesting journey, taking a little longer than it might usually as this was due to a number of roads being blocked off, some with heavily armed police stationed at the road blocks! This particular day the Israeli Prime Minister, Benjamin Netanyahu was in Sydney on his very first visit to Australia. Security was paramount!

Arriving back at the hotel and waving Apollo and Ann-Marie farewell, we headed for the hotel's bar for a very welcome nightcap, following a fairly full day of travel and all that entails.

The following morning, after a good night's sleep, we ventured down to breakfast. As we reached the ground floor the opening of the lift doors showed that a rather large liner was berthed right in front of us. However, it wasn't the Elizabeth, but the Queen Mary 2, both Cunard ships being in Sydney at the same time. Elizabeth, the smaller sister (just a little smaller), being relegated to the other side of the Harbour, but at anchor in the waterway, not docked due to a lack of berthing space for her size, with her larger 'stable mate' pulling rank and pinching the space outside the Ocean Terminal. They were to swap places the very next day, when Elizabeth was scheduled to be embarking guests.

Striding past this special view we arrived at the hotel's restaurant for breakfast and the outlook was somewhat gloomy, with grey skies and pouring rain greeting us at our window table. However, we could still see the ship's bow, a very large bow of the Mary right in our view.

Although the rain was beating against our window, the Maitre 'd was at least amusing and entertaining with a few jokes and observations of the day ahead. The United Nations of waiting staff were all very friendly and helpful, as usual for a Park-Hyatt establishment.

The omelette I ordered for breakfast was acceptable, although not quite up to B.K.'s standard and omelettes are always my gauge for the chef's 'take' on the rest of the menus. Although it is fair to note here that, quite often at breakfast there will be a separate "breakfast chef" operating and not the Head Chef!

This simple dish of an omelette was something that was a judgment point in the movie of a couple of years' ago, "The One Hundred Foot Journey", with Helen Mirren.

She was interviewing a new chef for a position in her restaurant and gauging his credentials by asking him to prepare and cook an omelette. A simple task, but not always achieved with greatness!

However, my long black coffee that morning was very acceptable and a second cup was taken, before vacating to the lounge to await a slowing of rain and wind, now showing signs of improvement across the Harbour, with improved vision of the Opera House 'Sails'. Also, the full top section of decks of the Queen Mary could now be seen above the Overseas Terminal building in our foreground.

Following breakfast, an umbrella was acquired from the Concierge as it was decided we would taxi across to Double Bay, an area we were familiar with, to wander the, 'up market' selection of boutiques and then have a relaxing lunch. This would be followed by a trip to the local Woolworth's store to buy a few 'necessities' to take on board ship, such as quality facial tissues, mouthwash, hairspray, (not for me) and small bottles of water for drinking when out traveling.

Oh, and we also visited one of my favourite destinations, which was directly next door to the Woolworth store, Dan Murphy's.

Here we purchased two bottles of good Champagne to also take on board. Two bottles of wine being our allowed limit to accompany us up the 'gang plank'.

Once on board we also discovered two bottles of sparkling had been placed in our cabin, one already on ice. However, these were cheap and NOT cheerful bubbly, which would have been better poured down the sink!

These shortcuts always frustrate me. Why place two, very ordinary bottles of bubbly in your room, which are not going to impress your client, when one, good quality bottle of Champagne, at probably not much more in cost, would be more impressive.

Our weekend reading was already covered with papers provided by the hotel... together with a couple of magazines, once again 'acquired' from the Qantas lounge back in Brisbane…so, once on board tomorrow we could put our feet up and relax.

Gaining access to the ship was reasonably straight forward that late Sunday morning, with a car from the hotel driving us the 200 meters down the road, saving us the possible embarrassment of tripping over on the Boardwalk with half a dozen bags in tow, if we had walked over as previously planned.

And anyway, arriving in a stretched limo with an Audi badge on the grill and the young driver assisting you with your cases, impresses your fellow travelers no end ... and all complimentary too! Thank you, Park Hyatt.

Following the completion of the usual forms and handing over both our passports and providing relevant credit card details (for any on-board purchases...read beverages here) and then smiling for the camera for more security procedures, it was off up the stairs and heading for the ship's stairwell and directly into the ship's own security entry point.

Placing our small bags on the lead in to the scanning apparatus, making sure no "banned" items are concealed.

My sturdy and always carried on holidays, Swiss Army Knife, presented to security personally this time, to ensure no issues like our previous trip when our cases got held up for several hours and Security got their knickers in a twist over a, "concealed weapon", (my Swiss Army Knife, which I prefer to call a, Swiss Army Tool), in one of our suitcases. A rather silly situation, that pissed me off completely over this non-event.

Anyway, this day we passed this point with no issues, knife checked, blade less than the 50 mm allowance, so given approval to proceed and we were then directed to the lifts which would propel us to the 6th floor, leading us to our previously chosen cabin.

Our cabin had the same layout as previously experienced on a cruise we completed two years earlier, reasonably spacious, about ten mtrs. x three mtrs., with sufficient room for a king size bed, although nowhere near as big as the one at the Park-Hyatt. A lounge area consisting of settee, side arm chair and small coffee table, plus two T.Vs. were provided, one pointing toward the lounge area and the other facing the bed. Toward the entry door was the ensuite bathroom, with access via the small wardrobe section. This bathroom was of course definitely not as big as the Park Hyatt's!

There was a smallish bath, with shower over, a hand basin, with shelf under and a toilet suite, with "air-flush" disposal system, which 'sucked' the waste matter away in a rather loud 'wooooshhh' when you pushed the appropriate button on the wall. In fact, you could probably go to the toilet, have a shave at the basin and soak your feet in the bath, all in one move it was so compact. However, it was an adequate 'wet area'. Having surveyed the room and confirmed it was the same layout as before, we awaited our main luggage to appear. We didn't have to wait very long.

Our three large suitcases, arrived a short time later, placed in the corridor along-side our cabin. These were quickly retrieved by me and hauling them into our room, leaving them closed to enable us to get quickly away to our designated dining room for a welcome lunch.

At the restaurant entrance we had a sincere welcome by our designated Maitre 'd, Raul and his second in charge, Julian and pleasantries were exchanged. However, while we were eager to know where our allocated table was, more importantly we wished to acquire some, "Intelligence" on the other members on our table, as there were four other dinner guests, six in total on the table including us. So, questions were asked about our fellow diners, as pre-warned is forearmed they say. Whilst we wouldn't really know our table companions until dinner, as we were the only ones seated for lunch, our station waiter Alex, a lady from Russia we learned, was more than pleased to give us her assessment on the rest of our dinner companions. I think she had obtained a good understanding of three of them, Margareta and Mr. and Mrs. Roberts, as these guests were all on the World Voyage and had been on the ship now for around two months, joining the ship in Southampton, following its' commencement in Hamburg, Germany, a couple of days before.

In her straight-talking Russian manner, Alex informed us that the English couple, Mr. and Mrs. Roberts (Dave & Linda), were very friendly and pleasant guests. The lady from Sweden, Margareta, was by her account, a somewhat demanding person who liked to have things her way, but...was "O.K". But, "definitely do not sit in this chair, (Alex pointed to the chair next to a window section), … because SHE (Margareta), would ask you to move". There was also a single gentleman at this table as well, but he disembarked in Sydney and our 'Russian Adviser' wasn't sure who would be replacing him and joining us...we would all have to wait until that single person appeared.

Now we know from experience that your dinner companions can either make your trip interesting and enjoyable or they can make you wish you'd never set foot on this particular ship and you were contemplating jumping overboard.

When we were first on this ship about five years earlier, our first trip to the dining room was not the best of experiences.

That first evening's dinner, me suitably dressed in the required jacket and tie, my wife in the suggested, "cocktail style dress", we ventured to the eleventh floor Princess Grills Restaurant, our designated dining room for our entire trip. Upon entering we were greeted by the Maitre 'd who checked his list for our allotted table and after a few minutes of 'assessment', finally directed us to table no. 124.

Now I'm not sure if this direction was his form of a joke or because I wasn't wearing the right tie, but he placed us on a table of eight, right in the center of the dining room.

However, there was only one other guest already seated there. In fact, there was only this one other guest seated with us at this location all through dinner. We were soon to understand why. We were seated with a Mr. Green and we soon came to realize that Mr. Green, poor soul, had dementia and in recent weeks had been made a widower, with the death of his wife of many years. In a dinner time period of around one & a half hours, Mr. Green told us the same story ten times, at regular intervals.

As you can imagine, the thought of spending the best part of four weeks having dinner with Mr. Green every evening was chilling, so the Maitre 'd, who I now had negative vibes about, was approached and given the "Kenchington stare". I requested that we be relocated to another table, for the remainder of the trip!

And this is where you can either get lucky and placed at a table with like-minded people, or the Maitre 'd gets annoyed and places you on a table of non-English speaking Japanese, who although are very happy, smiling people, do not understand a word you say and laugh a lot.

However, our move was a good one to a table of six and our new dining companions of four, were two couples from England. One couple who actually lived on the Isle of Man, the lady, English, a writer I believe, her husband was American and the other couple from Hertfordshire, Barry and Ann. We got on with very well with Barry and Ann and spent a number of times in their company, including trips on-shore and the last time my wife and I were in England we were invited to stay the night at their large English Manor style home and we enjoyed a wonderful two days of eating, drinking and talking.

Even now, several years later, we still exchange the odd communication via e-mail and hopefully, after this Covid nightmare, we will again join them on a cruise, somewhere in the world.

Now, today on the Queen Elizabeth, the current Maitre 'd Raul, who was new to us, placed us on this very same table as the one we were sat with Barry and Ann, so we presumed this was a good omen and at least, a good start.

Leaving our Sydney berth that evening, around six o'clock, we attended the, "Leaving Sydney Party", up on the 9th level, with Veuve Clicquot Champagne flowing (if you paid for it) and the on-board, American band 'Changes', playing and singing a number of 'oldies'.

As I mentioned previously, this was one of those experiences that money just can't buy. Sailing away past the Sydney Harbour Bridge, the Opera House next door, all lit up (even though it was still quite light) and a great number of us dancing to the familiar 'oldies' while slurping champagne and soaking up the moment. Fantastic!

Dinner Table Companions.

That first evening at dinner we arrived at our designated table a little after seven p.m., having danced a little at the, 'Leaving Sydney Party'.

We were the first there, so we waited in anticipation. Our allotted waiter, Alexandra or Alex as she preferred, was awaiting all her guests and was convivial in her welcome.

Pleasantries were exchanged on the usual topic, the weather, which had been raining most of the day and Alex had not had the opportunity of getting off the ship, so was a little despondent. She was also a little depressed as her boyfriend, working somewhere on the ship, was getting off soon and on his 'allotted ', shore leave. So, Alex would be 'alone'!

Our conversation was cut short by the arrival of our first dining companions, Mr. and Mrs. Roberts, or Dave and Linda, as we were told to call them.

Dave and Linda were from Manchester and I was immediately reminded of the movie Shirley Valentine, when Shirley (played by the actress, Pauline Collins) refers, in a derogatory manner, to two of her fellow travel companions, (in a Manchester Brogue) as, "Jeanette and Dougie from Manchester", who she found annoying.

Anyway, Linda and Dave were not annoying, but interesting people, with Dave telling us that he was a chef for a couple of years and later worked in the motor vehicle business, and mainly associated with Mercedes Benz, for around thirty years. In later years his business (although he was now retired), was selling secondhand trucks to the South Americans and South Africans and anyone else for that matter, after first refurbishing them. Obviously a very profitable business and his eldest daughter had now taken over the business.

Anyway, the next person to join our growing throng was the Swedish lady Margareta, who spoke very good English, with virtually zero accent. It turned out that Margareta was brought up in America and had spent many years in later life traveling between the two countries and was now based in Sweden.

We learned early on that Margareta was a fairly straight-talking lady and wanted you to know her opinion on everything, whether you wanted to know it or not. She was getting off at Kobe in Japan, but only for a week, to catch-up with one of her sons who would be flying in, especially to see his mum and spend a week with her. Margareta would then be rejoining the ship on its' planned return to Kobe, a week later. Margareta was, together with Dave and Linda, doing the whole World trip and all had been on board at that stage about two months, as previously mentioned. So, we were definitely the new guys and were being scrutinized every bit as much as we were scrutinizing them.

Our last and also new traveling dinner companion arrived, a lady whose name was Joan, a single lady, now retired and living in Canberra having moved from Sydney. Joan was a little quiet to begin with and was no doubt a little overawed by her dinner companions who to her, were all at the table and 'together' before she got there.

Joan was the only non-drinker amongst us, with all the others ordering white and red each evening. Hic!

Joan was also travelling to Kobe, a trip of around fifteen days from our commencement in Sydney. She was then dis-embarking (sometimes known as 'de-barking', sounds rather like a dog having its' bark removed) and spending a few days in Japan before returning to her life in Canberra.

So, the table 104 was now complete with six occupants for at least the next two weeks.

At the end of that first evening's dinner, we at least felt that the 'mix' of table 104 was ...O.K.

Sailing out through Sydney Heads that evening we were feeling quite relaxed and enjoying the breeze on the outside deck, heading for Brisbane, to arrive the day after tomorrow. Time enough to settle into the environment and re-acquaint ourselves with the ship and its' various important on-board 'destinations', like the bars, the eateries and ... the laundry.

The laundry, actually one on most floors where 'residents' resided, was always a busy location and getting a vacant washing machine or the ironing board was like planning a military operation. Strategy, timing, maneuvers, even deception, (hanging an, "out of order" sign on the door) and generally advancing rather than retreating, was paramount. Ten days without washing your smalls was the absolute limit, by then you were becoming desperate and the, "out of order sign" definitely a considered option!

Other shipmates seemed to hang about in the narrow space of the laundry, an overall size of probably around, 1.5 Mtrs. x 4 Mtrs. People would just stand there and watch their, 'smalls' go round in circles in the washer, presumably nothing better to do.... I felt like saying, "Go away, go get a coffee or something", rather than just cram into that small space, especially if someone was ironing. Half the room was then already taken up, especially if the ironer happened to have a whole basket full still to be given the heat treatment, nearly always placed on the floor next to them and you fell over it...Aghh.

It wasn't until Monday, a whole week plus, into our journey and just prior to lunch, that a washing machine was found vacant...YES! We were in there 'like Flynn', (whoever he was), one large bag only, the "whites", the "darks" would have to wait. So, whites it was, some items "ten days old" by now, crammed into the machine, dials turned and on-switch pushed, water whirred, we were, 'all systems go', the dining room our next stop.

Following a reasonably shorter lunch period we returned to transfer the wash into the dryer. Of course, we were too late, someone had already removed our belongings from the machine and placed them into a plastic basket. Hmmm, someone had handled my Calvin Klein undies...we were assured by the lady now occupying our washing machine, that "all had been retrieved, nothing left in the washer, so not to worry"! Hmmm, five minutes too late, someone had possibly 'contaminated' my boxer shorts. Still, the heat from the dryer, which was just about to be commandeered by us, would dispel any bugs, I was sure!

Call me paranoid if you wish, but I don't like just anyone handling my undies!

Well drying complete, ironing of shirts and one pair of trousers was now the priority and as luck would have it, I secured the iron without resorting to un-armed combat, no takers of the board! So, four shirts and one pair of cotton trousers were given the heat treatment.

This position taken by me has previously brought offers of marriage from women entering the laundry and exclaiming, "oh, a man who irons, are you married?"

However, I had noticed on this trip that more men were ironing, some possibly single men, but more married men, I was suitably impressed, even though women were no longer ' swooning' over me! ... "What's that my darling wife, oh yes, I'll iron your blouse next"!

Our day of washing was really a necessity, having spent around three hours the previous day on shore in the PNG port of Alotau. The heat and high humidity of the day was such that our clothes were as if we had jumped into the swimming pool.

After a couple of hours sight-seeing in the port of Alotau, we returned to the ship, whereupon entering our cabin our clothes were discarded to the floor and one after the other, we jumped into the shower to refresh, Ahhhh…

Our abandoned wardrobe being added to the already, bursting at the seams, laundry bag, 'screaming' at us to be taken to the laundry!

Our short period on PNG was our first time here and of interest, although anticipated from our knowledge of this region gained from T.V. programs shown over the years and similar visits made by us, to islands such as Pago Pago and Samoa.

We had booked the 'two hour' tour of the local area, which of course was nearing three hours by the time we got back to the ship, being on 'local' time, no rush! We were actually in a "convoy of buses". I use this term loosely, as our mode of transportation were vans, although with windows, seating around ten or twelve (much like a maxi-taxi), but they appeared borrowed from some of the local businesses going by the sign writing on the outside of them. These vans were of varying quality, with most having no air conditioning and some having seen better times for sure, our particular van having the remnants of Betel Nut chewing, with blood like stains on the upholstery. Betel Nut chewing being a local pastime, giving the locals red to black teeth making them look a little like Dracula's assistants!

Our bus was also sporting a rather large gash in the top of the front driver's side tyre, a gash of about a foot in length. I did point this hazard out to our particular driver, who carried out a brief inspection with a fellow driver, but he just shrugged and jumped aboard and off we went…

There was one amusing incident at the very commencement of this short trip, at least it appealed to my sense of fairness. There were several, possibly sixty of us, awaiting our transportation to arrive and a Japanese couple, obviously 'eager' not to be left behind, walked past us all making their way to the front of the 'queue'.

This mean looking move proved to backfire on them though. Now at the front of the queue, they were loaded onto the first van and this particular transport vehicle was the very worst looking, quite dilapidated with rust everywhere, no air con, torn upholstery and the engine belching clouds of smoke. So, serve them right.

Once we were all aboard our various transport vehicles, this convoy of ramshackle 'buses' took off, hazard lights on and we ambled slowly along the only street and up a hill to our first stop.

The Local Welcome Team of Music and Dancing

Some local, 'wealthy resident', with a large home, built mostly of timber, sitting on a couple of acres, by the look of it, had allowed us to alight and check out the fabulous view over the bay. The houses on the hill being the very best in this region, we were told, but houses still of a standard design in our opinion.

There was a brief speech provided on the area and in particular an overview of the war period and the Japanese invasion, which was of course the most notable thing probably ever to have happened here and certain members of our party (the Japanese that is), switched off and walked off in another direction.

But in the main the majority of our Japanese fellow travelers were very polite and friendly, as we have always found them to be personally.

Following this brief stop to view the bay and surrounds, we once again jumped aboard our designated bus and off, back down the hill, avoiding several free roaming dogs.

We were headed toward a local school which was partially residential, to be given a guided tour. This was following a selection of pupils, in a small group, singing their National Anthem. These young teenagers singing their country's National song, mostly seemed bored, some not even knowing the words I think, just 'miming' and relying on their fellow songsters to give it their all. Following this we commenced a tour of their school and on our particular tour, our guide was Romany, a young local schoolboy, a quite eloquent young fellow, parading us through his classrooms, via the open-air passages. Virtually all were timber construction buildings, with wooden desks, chalkboards and solid dusters, reminiscent I felt of most of us travelers' school days, of years gone-by.

Romany was asked what he would like to do when he left school and he replied that he was mostly interested in electrical engineering, so would endeavour to work in this industry. We

were generally impressed with all our 'tour guides', who a number indicated they wanted to be doctors or work in the medical profession when they finished their schooling.

Following the brief tour of the classrooms we all ventured across to the 'sportsground'. Not so much green grass, but a mixture of pebbles and some sort of tufted green plant, which housed a number of open huts with two in particular housing local 'performers', ready to perform for their new guests.

One group of ladies dressed in traditional grass skirts and feathers, a couple with their breasts fully exposed, with seemingly not a care in the world, acting out some sort of dress making skill, with dried grasses. In one other hut to the left of this was a larger group of mostly men and around six women, again in traditional costume, eagerly awaiting their turn to sing and dance for us.

However, I think this might have been the 'B Team' as they didn't appear to know all the moves and would often bump into each other while moving in certain directions.

This group plus the other team obviously being put together for the, tourists off the big boat landing today!

This is a very poor country and you couldn't help feeling for their plight, but they appeared happy with their lot, even though they had no money and no government welfare support.

Our PNG guide assured us they lived an enjoyable life, some homes even with no electricity we were informed but, as also endorsed by our guide, they never received an electric bill!

Back on the bus, we headed the short distance, slowly back to the ship and back to normality, leaving behind a happy bunch of islanders that for them tomorrow would be, just another day.

Cruising ...

That evening at dinner was an informal dress evening. This means you don't have to wear a dinner suit and Dickie Bow

Milne Bay, Papua New Guinea, with Queen Elizabeth at dock.

Tie, but you still have to wear a jacket, if you're a man that is. Although tie is optional.

Typically… British, don't you know!

Anyway, me being an Aussie...now and quite happy to not wear a tie and I don't really like wearing a bow tie, although I do have a couple (different colours) with me, but I mostly gave up wearing a bow tie when I stopped being a waiter over 50 years ago!

Of course, my wife likes to see me looking like a penguin, but I avoid this style of dress if possible.

Most of the diners that evening wore no tie, it was after all, quite a hot and humid day, so a very good reason to have open shirt only... oh, plus the jacket of course. No jacket means no dinner! The Maitre' d will not allow you access to the dining room!

Having around 2000 guests on board you would think it would be a little crowded, but being the size of the Queen Elizabeth, you rarely feel over-crowded. The various daily activities also happening, from Lectures by qualified speakers to dancing classes, with the on-board dance couple, who are remarkably agile and physically fit, or to Bridge playing, (cards that is), aided this feeling of not being crowded.

I found it interesting that eleven hundred 'shipmates' got off in Sydney, de-barked, woof, woof. However, eleven hundred new travelers got on, with a similar situation occurring in Brisbane, with a turnover of around 400 guests there.

So, within two days, three quarters of all the guests changed. And I'm pleased to say that at least 25 percent of us were now Australian. No language barrier, with the balance of us being mostly, American, English and Japanese, who no doubt would alight, when back in their own country.

You do find though, that there are a few, "strange ones" amongst you, like the American lady we've encountered on previous trips aboard this ship. A seasoned traveler for sure, she must be around eighty, but wears this rather tall and rounded, coiffured wig, no doubt endeavouring to make herself appear thirty years younger! In reality though, we consider her to look more like royalty from the 1700's, especially wearing her particular face make-up to match and also sporting large fake eye lashes... Hmmm.

Then there's the couple that have a very big age gap by the look of it. He looks about sixty, his partner a young, attractive lady of probably mid- thirties...half his luck. They're actually in the cabin next to ours and I'm sure I heard some 'screams' coming through the adjoining wall the other morning!!

We also have a few Gay Couples on board and one particular couple loves to dance together, the elder partner probably in his late sixties and his partner possibly fiftyish. But hey, you should see them on the dance floor, wow, like a pair of teenagers both of them...where do they get all that energy?

The evening the D.J. played the Abba selection they were up on the dance floor, dancing the steps and punching the air in step to the beat.

Yes, our traveling shipmates came in all shapes, sizes and looks. The Japanese man sat on the dinner table behind us reminded me of the bad guy from a James Bond movie and the older lady on the table to my left was a dead ringer for Mrs. Bucket from the comedy T.V. Series, One foot in the Grave. Not that I watched that particular show, only seeing the ABC's adverts for it. And I was sure that I spotted Freddy Mercury the other day. However, I later discovered that this person was from the band on board, called the Bohemians, who played all the old Queen songs in a one-night show! And, they were bloody good!

The other day at morning coffee I could have sworn that Pauline Hanson was on board, the 'red' hair, the same eye liner... and then on the other table next to us, an older lady looking exactly like the lady who sits at the end cash register station at our local Coles Supermarket. We always have a joke with her when we join her register queue, especially when we have purchased one of our favourite items, a small Spatchcock, which she believes is far too small and needs fattening up a bit...well her double was definitely at the next table.... Six days at sea is warping my mind.

Yes, six days…I think that should read, "daze at sea" and being currently on the sixth day at sea and no land in sight, a little boredom has set in, with no shore leave.

All we seem to do is eat; breakfast, lunch and dinner, plus afternoon tea is a favourite, very English, with scones, jam and cream! I know I've gained a couple of extra kilos!

We do occasionally listen to a lecture or watch one on the T.V., which was recorded the day prior, but apart from those few things, over the past couple of days it has been raining, with gusty winds, so not much fun walking around deck three. Although, the weather was kind the day of the, International Women's Day, which was celebrated on board with several ladies and some men (dressed as ladies), walking ten times around deck three, this equaling five kilometres. I did do a little walking, well only about 50 metres, taking photographic evidence of my wife, who completed this great effort for charity. She slept well that night, despite the swell and gusty conditions.

The International Women's Day also saw the ship's Captain, Aseem Hashmi, dressed in a pirate's hat, dark shorts and T-shirt, walking with the ladies and providing great support and a few funny photo opportunities to the onlookers.

The captain is a very pleasant man with a terrific sense of humour and was quite possibly the most down to earth captain I had experienced in our few years of cruising.

He was born in Coventry, England where he still lives with his wife and two daughters. Following his time at a local Technical College he embarked on a career with British Airways becoming a pilot, before changing course…no pun intended … and moving quickly through the ranks in the Cunard Line.

The one thing that I found funny was that in every talk or morning statement made by Captain Hashmi, he would call his Charge, "The Queen Elizabuth" and his pronunciation of Cunard as well was 'different', calling it CUN…ARD.

Ah well, we all have our little foibles!

Well today, land is in sight and we're heading for the port of Naha, Okinawa our first port of call for six days. This Japanese Island, (well Japanese since 1972 that is, after domination by American Forces since 1945), we have visited a few years before. Then, we visited the historical military sections, including the World War Two tunnels on the coast, where Japanese soldiers awaited the landing of American forces. This trip is not for the faint hearted or those who suffer claustrophobia and for me that day I had to remove myself from those deep, long tunnels, feeling quite overwhelmed and 'entombed'. Apparently, many Japanese soldiers committed suicide while positioned in these tunnels, bullet holes still evidenced in the walls. This history piece does not place the Japanese hierarchy in a 'flattering position'.

So, this time on our Island visit my wife and I decided on a short tour, albeit 5 hours in duration and we went to visit a Botanic style park titled, The Royal Park (which our guide called, "the Loyal Park", as the 'R " letter would appear difficult for some of them to master). Following on from this, we travelled on to an older style Japanese village, situated further down the coast, about hour from our ship. The village itself was all re-constructed, we were informed, with gardens and a natural lake being our first stop, although not stunning and not the best piece of landscape we've seen. It was also pouring with rain and the pathways through this village were not only muddy but poorly surfaced, it was not fun.

Then it was back on the coach for a very arduous hour and a half drive through heavy traffic back to the ship. The motorway nearby not being utilized by our coach, no doubt due to additional cost of the toll, the coach company would have to pay. On the coach ride home, we had time to reflect on this second venue, the 'village'. It was basic and not terribly enlightening and of course, while at this venue we were, once again 'entertained' with the local 'villagers' doing a, drum dance routine. However, this did lead into an entertaining fifteen minutes with a long and very hairy, golden 'dragon' appearing with a rather square, fearsome face snapping at the visitors and making us all laugh. Fifteen minutes of silliness formally captured by the photographers amongst us on their i-phones mostly, before re-boarding our coach. Heading back to the ship, I was looking forward to a very welcome, large glass of red!

The next day was another on the high seas and typical, this day we have excellent weather with blue sky and sunshine, where was this yesterday when we were trudging around and getting soggy.

The following day we were early into our next port of call, Kobe, arriving around 6.00 a.m. Here we were to have another large turnover of shipmates.

Around 850 getting off and a similar number getting on, we were informed by Alex. Our new travelers being mostly Japanese tourists, doing a week round trip, as we would return to Kobe in seven days. Our dining companions, Joan and Margareta, both leaving us, only Margareta to return in seven days, following her re-union with her son, as previously mentioned. Joan was having about five days in Kobe, doing a few trips out each day, before flying back to Canberra.

Today in Kobe we had another trip organized, a whole nine hours, heading to Kyoto (once the capital of Japan) and visiting three Temples... Grreeaat, my wife's idea...But it did include lunch, which turned out to be a very good Japanese lunch of many smaller dishes. Salmon and Squid Sashimi, Tempura prawn and vegetables, rice of course, pickled veg, Tofu in a hot soup and several other items. I'm not sure what they all were, but they tasted delicious and I did not get food poisoning...always a benefit!

Our tour though established my long held believe that, once you've seen one Temple, you've seen them all. And I was very much supported on this trip, with the lady traveler behind me in the coach lamenting, "a Temple too far". By the time we arrived at the final destination this statement was immediately trumped by a joker further back in the coach saying, "yes and a gift shop too far as well"!

However, although a long and tiring day it was made quite enjoyable by our tour guide, a Japanese gentleman of about sixty-five, apparently a grandfather and now semi-retired. He told us that he had been a businessman for several years in the steel

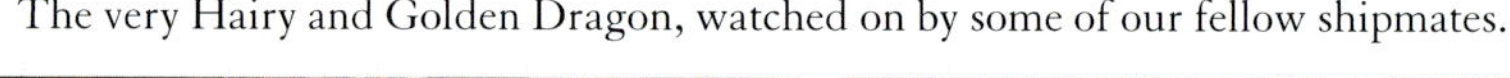

The very Hairy and Golden Dragon, watched on by some of our fellow shipmates.

industry, including about ten years spent working in the U.S. This explained his very good English, although it was "L's" he had a problem with, given over to "R's". He was quite knowledgeable and gave interesting commentary on our trip, with many funny comments, making us all laugh.

He was at pains to point out that he had worked in the STEEL business and not the STEAL business. One statement he made was amusing to me, "Cherry Brossom come into full broom in two week"! This statement referencing the numerous Cherry trees planted along the roadside…as well as in pretty much, all green spaces.

Our tour guide did however get a little political on our return journey to the ship. Standing in the coach aisle and making the statement that he would like to make us aware of two concerns he had about his country.

His first concern was that, currently Japan had a population of around 127 million people. However, due to the present death rate,

Cherry blossom trees are almost everywhere.

of about one million, three hundred thousand per year and with the current birth rate of only around a million, meant that by 2048 (his calculation), Japan's population would drop to less than one hundred million!

He commented that young people were getting married later, average age now around thirty-one, whereas in his day, young people would be mostly married in their mid-twenties, like himself was. Indeed now, they often had their babies later still, due to economic issues of one partner having to give up work. I would assume that this observation was not only common to the people of Japan.

His other concern was the financial state of his country. Apparently, Japan had a GDP (gross domestic productivity) of around, five hundred trillion Yen. However, the country had borrowings of double this at, one thousand trillion Yen and unless something was done about raising more income, they would never be able to repay this debt. Coupled with this he made the comment that the lower population figure would include around a third of it being over sixty-five, who would no longer contribute taxes! I also shared his concern by this stage.

Following this venting of 'anguish ', he returned to his front passenger seat and allowed us to contemplate his statements.

Our Tour Guide also made one other statement earlier that day which was, that you could buy a home in Japan by first putting down around a thirty percent deposit and then mortgage the balance of the house purchase with a one percent mortgage. Yes, one percent!

It would appear that there is a need for the Japanese financial institutions to review their income streams, if they are to reduce their country's debt levels!

I for one contemplated all of this while looking out the coach window as we sped along the motorway at the limit of 80 KPH. Although by now dark outside, we were entering the more built-up areas, with street lighting and I was reminded how cramped these cities were that we had so far visited.

So many medium high-rise units, so close together, with virtually no space between each building, but occasionally you sited, illuminated sports stadiums of soccer, basketball and the Japanese favourite on larger sections, golf ranges. These mostly all placed under the raised sections of the busy motorway, passing overhead or to the immediate side of them, space being of a premium.

We were also informed later that, Japan had some thousands of islands, but only four larger ones made up the majority of the known country. Of these, sixty five percent was mountainous and of the more level parts, fifteen percent was given over to agriculture and only five percent was utilized for general living... not sure what they did with the remaining fifteen percent. Maybe rivers and waterways perhaps! Anyway, this does explain why so many high-rise buildings are evident.

When we arrived back to our 'steel home' there were still a number of flag wavers and musicians at the port and welcoming us back, but also to wave us goodbye, when sailing out of the port a little later that evening.

It was a great finish to our day out and reinforced our feeling of friendship felt with these local people.

This morning we awoke to a very pleasant day weather wise, as we pulled into the port of Kagoshima, with high palm trees lining the surrounding wharf area. We also had a local brass band containing around fifteen musicians, all dressed in crisp white uniforms, with peaked caps, looking very official. There was a big welcome party at the dock, apparently including the local Mayor and dignitaries and many flags flying and a jolly good display it all was.

There were, what seemed like, bus-loads of people all waving and smiling and welcoming us to their town.

Kagoshima is the capital city of Kagoshima Prefecture at the South Western tip of the island of Kyushu in Japan. Apparently, we were told, that this city has been nicknamed the, "Naples of the Eastern World", for its' bay location and the very large and magnificent looking, Sakurajima Volcano on the very close, adjoining island.

Transport in the city includes trams, quite like Melbourne trams and if you really want to get somewhere more quickly you can always use the Shinkansen, better known as, The Bullet Train.

The city and surrounding area were the best in appearance of all the cities so far visited and we were booked on a half day tour which included the magnificent, 300- year-old Sengan-en Garden, which had the wonderful backdrop of Mount Sakurajima and Kinko Bay.

We also had a few trees in "brossom" sorry, blossom and certain fern trees, giving off a little pollen and many locals were wearing masks, with our guide saying that this was often due to not wanting to breathe in the pollen from the Cedar trees, which also grew extensively in the region.

This outing was a quite relaxing day of walking through gardens, parkland and trees and the fine weather ensuring a very pleasant region was presented at its' very best.

Returning to the ship in the late afternoon we were again surprised to see so many locals at the portside. The associated car park was now full, with a big group of dancing girls performing at one end of the wharf and a booming band of big drums performing at the other end of the wharf.

As it neared our departure time the crowds grew still further with flags waving. The sounds of each band grew louder and there was excitement aplenty. There were dancing girls and now various musicians playing differing instruments, as if competing to be heard above each other. It was as if they had never seen a big

cruise liner before. And, where did these people work? There were literally hundreds of people gathered along the wharf and also on the adjacent rocky point to wave us off.

Some being there a whole afternoon possibly even arriving in the morning and making a 'day out' of it.

We returned the waving from the sanctuary of our cabin's balcony, but not for long as it was bitterly cold by now and how the various groups down below us on the wharf, with skimpy outfits on didn't freeze was quite amazing to us.

That evening however, I developed a streaming nose and a cough and I was thankful that our, Aloe Vera tissues we had bought in Cairns, were on hand.

I was not in a good state and put my condition down to Hay Fever, from our day out to the gardens and was suddenly wishing I had also been using the face mask.... after all, we did bring a couple with us, but they were still in the suitcase!

I did however venture to the dining room for dinner, but with a pocketful of tissues on hand and a couple of trips to the Gents to blow my nose and wash my hands and I was not too much of a nuisance to my fellow diners. I also think that large brandy in the bar before dinner helped a little!

One of the many welcome and goodbye bands that greeted us.

Waving goodbye from the locals. Many very friendly faces and bands playing.

Fushimi, Kyoto, Japan

Our Entry to Busan Port, South Korea

The next morning, following a peaceful crossing of the Korean Straits we arrived in the port city of Busan, formerly known as Pusan. This was the second largest city in, "The Republic of Korea", we were informed (which meant, South Korea), second city to the capital, Seoul.

The sail into the port was quite pleasant and its' visual status was probably the best so far, in this Asian region. There were bay views and various high-rise buildings in groups, but with more space between, unlike the Japanese territory so far visited. The Japanese city structures afforded no real space between the high

rises and often these buildings were of variable quality in their appearance. So, this presentation of Busan this morning was a pleasant change.

Thankfully my sniffles and runny nose had abated, so only a 24hour thing and both I and my fellow dining companions were pleased. However, this day was not to be my best…

It started late with us arriving into port just over an hour later than our scheduled time. This being put down to leaving the previous port of Kagoshima late, due to the necessary customs and immigration review on leaving the Japanese sector. We were running overtime, with some travelers saying that this delay was also due because two ladies were very late getting back on the ship that afternoon and completing this legal requirement.

So, not only were we late, but our day then progressed into farce, with the Korean immigration personnel coming on board to check our passports.

Large groups of us, mostly standing in the theatre area and waiting our turn to proceed to this passport review. And even when being given the go-ahead to move out of the theatre to go to the passport review, we then joined a very long queue, making a very slow walk to the sector where this was all taking place.

Those of us on the booked and PAID FOR coach trips, were held up by poor organization of this passport review with, "every man and his dog" being allowed through, making the PAYING tourists nearly two hours late for the start of their trips, with our time lines completely out.

So eventually getting on our coach for our much-anticipated tour, starting with the markets, this late start created a little debate and it was decided an adjustment should be made. The tour guide suggesting we head straight for our planned luncheon, as it was now 1.00 pm!

And here it got worse for me…

The lunch was a buffet, arranged at a local hotel, which was in the design of a local Buddhist Temple with several tiers of Pagodas, with typical Asian Dragons and Snakes adorning several sections of the roof. In the dining section one 'joker' labeling this, "the get-out-of-my-way buffet" and the food, whilst looking good, certainly did not have the same eating quality as our previous outing.

Finishing lunch, I thought it a good idea to visit the loo, prior to our departure, as it could apparently be another hour and a half before alighting our coach at the next destination.

It was at this point that I must have upset the gods or the dragons (take your pick), because my trip to the 'Happy Room', (as our previous Tour Guide had called the Public Toilets), was not the experience of fondness!

The buffet eatery was now quite busy with three tour buses from the ship, having arrived one after the other, behind us.

All obviously realizing that the late start would now be better served by heading straight to lunch. This busier time saw more people heading to the 'Happy Room', so me, entering the busy gents, headed to the vacant cubicle. With both the lid and the

Our luncheon Hotel … and "Happy Room" stop …Not!

seat already lifted, I did my 'business' and searched for the 'flush' button.

Now... this is where the language barrier is sometimes a BIG hindrance. I don't know if you've ever viewed these larger than normal Asian toilet suites, with a fully operational electronic 'washing system', I hadn't until this trip. On the side of the basin, right next to the toilet was a square, plastic box with the word, 'Flush' on the top of the single button on said box. So, leaning slightly forward I pressed to flush.... all this did was to puff a spray of perfume straight into my face, now blurring my vision!

Not thwarted by this initial attempt to flush the bowl, I searched the six illuminated, 'flat' section of switches positioned directly along the side of the toilet bowl to find the 'flush' button. Now with slightly impaired sight the only square push button with a picture looking anything like flushing water, I pushed...A whirring sound was heard, I thought fantastic I got it right. I turned slightly to ensure success.

At this point a slim and angled plastic pipe, resembling a weapon, suddenly protruded from inside the toilet bowl and squirted a continuing blast of water at me, hitting me full in the chest.

It continued unabated, I was suddenly dumbstruck and wet.

Regaining my senses, I jumped out of the way of this 'hose pipe' and it continued, like a small water cannon, a stream of water now hitting the door behind me, running down it and pooling on the floor, heaps of it.

I regained my composure and avoiding the fearsome stream, I managed to kick shut the lid of the toilet with my foot. The water jet continued on inside the now closed lid. I managed to escape the cubicle, throwing open the door and stepping over the now rather deep puddle on the floor. I headed to the basins to wash my hands. In the background I could still hear the cascading water flowing inside the now lidded bowl.

As I finished the hand washing and endeavored to dry my shirt with paper towels, I could hear the water cannon go silent, the flow of water ceased, the whole room fell silent. Feeling rather foolish I quickly left and headed for the outdoors in an endeavour to get fresh air to my damp shirt and dry it out! Leaving the now, 'un-happy room' for some poor sod to tidy up after the silly Australian tourist.

Arriving outside to join my wife and our fellow travelers and me looking somewhat DAMP, I spent the next ten minutes explaining my 'Happy Room' moment, to the merriment from my fellow shipmates…Personally, I can't imagine what it would have been like to, "complete other business" in that public toilet and use that system to "clean you", the water flow was ferocious! Surely you would need a large towel to dry yourself afterwards.

Especially with that rather full-on system. Doesn't bear thinking about … move on. I avoided that type of toilet suite from then on!

Back on the coach it was decided by our tour guide that, due to our late start and the lunch stop first, we would now head to the general food markets and then a short walk away, onto the fish markets.

Following these stops, we would then proceed on to the main item of this day's tour, the Haedong Yonggungsa Temple.

On arrival at the entrance to the markets, about twenty minutes later, (not the hour and a half as previously suggested), we commenced our own individual walk around the shops and the many, many market stalls, along the large grid style of streets. The shops and associated stalls were selling anything and everything... none of which we either needed or wanted, but it was just good to stroll the streets and see how, "the rest of the world lives".

We had far too much time allocated for this stop, about an hour and a half, (maybe this was the reference to the, 'hour and a half', something obviously lost in translation). Half of this allotted time would have been quite sufficient.

We then re-grouped, all forty of us and our guide instructed us to walk in couples, much like school children I thought and we walked in a long line, back down the narrow market street to the main road, about five hundred meters away. Once across this busy road we were on the quayside and entering the very large fish markets.

Wow, more varieties and volume of fish in one market than I have ever seen in my life, some sea life alive and swimming in big tanks. But most of this remarkable collection, from large mackerel type species to medium size octopus and heaps of different sea life of all varieties and (in the words of John Cleese) were "dead, deceased and definitely not moving".

All were piled high and lying on plastic covered crates, having water continuously thrown over them by the stallholders. Maybe this was to make the 'stock' look 'fresh', but every single display was un-refrigerated!

Not a lot of HACCP* in evidence here.

We once again spent too much time in this area and my fellow shipmates/coach-mates, were getting restless, as we could all determine that the day was rapidly approaching 4 .30pm and we still had the Conference facility to visit. This was on the way to basically, the main event, the special Temple, which a large number of our party were wanting to take photos of, especially of the surrounding gardens, with it being right on the ocean front it would provide some extra special photos.

So, patience was running out and when we got to the Conference Centre, not too far away, mutiny almost occurred, as most of us did not want to go to a boring Conference building anyway. Voices were suddenly raised at the tour guide and people, some more vocal than others, were refusing to get off the bus, insisting we keep going, as darkness would be upon us before we got to the Temple and photographs would be out of the question.

Our tour guide persisted and got off the bus, leaving a majority behind, some staying on the bus moaning, some getting off, just to stretch their legs and a few getting off, wanting to see the Conference facility as we were now there.

* NB. HACCP...National Food Safety Guidelines, initials standing for: Hazzard Analysis and Critical Control Points. This mostly referred to the correct handling of food products and also the holding of those products at the correct temperatures. Either cold or hot. Under 4 degrees C. if refrigerated or above 65 degrees C. if hot.

However, unbeknown to us 'mutineers', when the guide was off the bus, she told the ones wanting to see the facility to, "wait, wait" and then apparently, she ran off down the road and disappeared. About fifteen minutes later, this group got back on the bus, all really annoyed that they had been abandoned on the footpath, not going anywhere.

Now, with most back on the bus, the grumbling became more pronounced and people were talking of seeing Cunard representatives when they were back on the ship and giving them a piece of their mind!

One gentleman we were speaking to, who was from New Zealand and probably in his mid to late seventies, respectable and well spoken, made the statement that, "his day had not been the best and it had gone haywire since the requirement to check through passport control". He then made further comment that, when he was back on board the ship he intended to, "relieve his negative day with a rest and then; ...get pissed tonight"!

He obviously did not have a good day.

After a short interlude, our tour guide reappeared, made her apologies for the 'error' of leaving the group standing on the path and asking them to wait and fumbled an excuse for this "misunderstanding". Her statement though was not received well and several passengers were literally shouting at her and I thought that she would burst into tears, but she did not. She just nodded to the coach driver and off we went, heading for the temple with the time now around five o'clock and the sun going down.

Arriving at the Temple perimeter about twenty minutes later we alighted from the coach, with some still mumbling and did manage to get into the temple and take photos. The daylight still quite good, but it was a big, steep trek down many uneven stone steps to get to the building itself from the coach park area. And as always, small, rubbishy souvenir shops, some mobile, were in proliferation in the prime spot and the visit was really not worth the effort.

So, after a twenty-minute 'photo shoot' by most of the bus passengers, we once again trudged back up the stone steps and loaded the bus up and took off up the road, heading for the ship, finally arriving in the dark, around 7.00pm… All of us fairly knackered and all, "Not happy Jan"!

For myself that evening, I concurred with that gentleman from New Zealand and a couple of large brandies seemed to fix me up!

Hiroshima

The following day was a 'sea day', the Elizabeth traversing the Kanmon Strait and heading, once again for Japan. There were many land sightings on the way through this region with a reasonably easy, tranquil and slow sail, through to one of the world's most notable cities.

On board this day not much out of the ordinary happening, just the usual… breakfast, lunch, afternoon tea and dinner... as usual.

However, the next day Saturday, after sailing through the Bungo Channel and around several islands, we arrived in Hiroshima. The largest city in the Chugoku region of western

Arriving in the port of Hiroshima

Honshu, the largest island of Japan and one of the four largest islands making up the major part of this country.

We had pre-booked a short, four-hour tour, consisting of a short ferry ride to Mijayima Island. This trip was as much for a visit to... yes, you've guessed it, another Temple, but more importantly, it would allow us a pleasant stroll along the seafront and through the small town, although once there, we realized the souvenir shops were still a big feature.

Following the short, ten-minute ferry ride across to the Island we walked along the seafront and 'shops', for the first twenty minutes with our Japanese tour guide. We could then see further along the Esplanade the usual orange sorry, vermillion coloured pole structure of the Temple ahead. We had already decided to break ranks and turn left and venture off through the narrow shopping streets by ourselves. Our tour guide had already given instructions, "to return to the ferry point at 1.00pm, should anybody wish to stroll by themselves". We therefore had about seventy-five minutes to ourselves.

Hiroshima is of course known as the city where the first atomic bomb was dropped in the second world war, on August 6th 1945, basically contributing to ending WW 2. Although a second atomic bomb dropped on Nagasaki, finally made the Japanese realize that the war should end.

A large number of our shipmates on this ship's cruise wanted to view the historical sites and the museum, we did not want to see "ground zero" or any other place associated with this monumental and historical event, as we had seen enough of these dreadful war memorials in Okinawa, when we were there a few years before.

Now, we were more interested to see positive points including, life as it is today, hence the very pleasant ferry ride to Mijayima Island.

Many Deer just roaming freely along the Esplanade on Mijayima Island.

Making our way along the 'promenade', we were surprised to see a number of young deer, just roaming the main street along the waterfront. They were freely strutting along, but if you were eating any type of food, they would target you endeavoring to receive any tidbit. Of course, these animals were a huge source of photographic material, with the very large number of both local and foreign tourists out walking this day.

Today was a Saturday and very busy, although it was no doubt busier than usual with this weekend being the start of a long weekend holiday in Japan.

There was one funny moment, just prior to us splitting from the main group heading to the Temple, when our smaller group of stragglers, bumped into a second touring group from the ship and a few stopped to chat.

One American lady, probably about sixty-five, who was stood next to me, was in full animated discussion with a couple, when without turning, she grabbed my arm and proceeded to stroke my 'jumpered limb' several times. When I stated that she would now have to marry me, she now turned to face me, realizing that I wasn't her husband, whom she thought she was stood next to. Following my comment, she apologized profusely and then said, "I can't marry you, I just got married". And she was then off to find the new husband who was now positioned at the stone wharf wall, looking across the bay. No doubt to stroke his arm instead.

It was just after this point that we were about to enter the said Temple. The main group of us descending down the stone steps, heading for the usual orange painted timber structures, of which there were an awful lot. My wife and I then made our getaway and strode off in the other direction for a little, very little, 'retail therapy'.

We strode down the narrow retail street, which was similar to many others we had seen and a few shops along this street we arrived at a shop selling T' shirts, where my wife bought a couple of appropriate children's shirts for our two grandsons.

After this we still had about forty minutes before the ferry left, so we found a small hotel in the street and ducked in and found a quiet lounge bar and enjoyed a cold Asahi beer each, … bliss!

Following a reverse of the trip over to the island, it was back to our steel ‘home’, arriving at 2.00pm, just enough time to squeeze in a light lunch in the Buffet and then a movie on the ‘telly’ and an afternoon snooze before....

You’ve guessed it, dinner.

At dinner there was some gossip... Apparently, there had been around six deaths on board, since the World Cruise had departed from Southampton. Someone jokingly asked, “was it food poisoning”?

I was reminded of our earlier trip on this ship, when the American on our table jokingly mentioned that a lady had died and they were all being asked to eat ice-cream, to enable enough room in the freezer to place the body!

I was thinking that you’d have to eat a bloody great deal of ice cream this time to accommodate six!

However, it is quite sad to think that a few had joined this cruise for a few weeks of enjoyment and no doubt seeing places that perhaps they had not seen before and then they pass away during the trip.

There were also whispers about two men having an argument and it developed into a punch-up and they were then apparently removed from the ship... and someone suggested that the wives of these two stayed on board! They were probably pleased to have some, “me-time”.

And one more piece of gossip… Allegedly, one shipmate, an American doctor had been arrested that day and handcuffed, by local police and taken off the ship.

The rumour being, that cocaine was found in his room. He was a ‘world traveler’ and the ship had stopped in, Columbia!!

Somebody had presumably seen something and reported it.

Fear suddenly struck me. I was instantly reminded of my wife’s HRT pills, a small square ‘sheet’ of about 100 mm square X 10mm deep, all cut into 5mm squares and wrapped in plastic, in a sealed plastic bag. These were left sitting on her bedside cupboard looking remarkably like...well, very small ice cubes.

I just hoped the housekeeper didn’t think they were something else!

I didn't fancy being carted off in handcuffs. A saving grace was, my wife had brought with her a copy of the doctor's prescription for these 'Ice' lookalikes. Not that I would know what this particular drug actually looked like.

Red wine being my preferred 'drug' of dependence!

Sunday morning and we are nearing the port of Kochi and will be arriving after breakfast, at about 10am.

This stop is new, as we were originally going to stay overnight in Hiroshima and the following day traverse the Japan Inland Sea (Kurishima Strait), between Hiroshima and Kobe. However, this proposed route had to be altered, due to a large fleet of Japanese fishing boats re-positioning in this narrow stretch of water and these boats could have delayed us.

So, this new stopover in Kochi was provided, reducing our stay to only one day in Hiroshima

This new stop was well worth it and far better in my opinion than traversing a narrow waterway. Once again, we were welcomed by literally hundreds of locals, including the mayor with a large brass band, dancing girls, uniformed school children singing and flag wavers of every description. And of course, this stop had only been arranged about two days before. A much-appreciated welcome by us shipmates for the considerable amount of preparation having been undertaken by the locals, in a very short period.

It was like being a ' Rock Star '... well I suppose it's not every day the Queen Elizabeth pulls into town.

Kochi is located on the Island of Shikoku and is the capital city of the Kochi Prefecture. The population here being around 350,000 and the region noted mostly for a castle, with the building of this commencing in 1601 and taking around ten years to complete. However, it burnt down 125 years later and a re-build took place in 1727 and a "periodic restoration" took place between 1948 and 1959. The other notable item of this region is a dish of seasoned and seared tuna fish called, Katsou Tataki… We didn't see either!

At this stop we had planned to have another coach tour, but following the debacle of our Korean trip we cancelled this and decided to just catch the free shuttle bus into the shopping centre to have the usual wander and a look.

Our shuttle bus brought us close to the Obiyamachi Shopping Arcade, with its' regular Sunday Street Markets, which are around one kilometer in length.

This weekend was still a long weekend holiday for the residents and the area was packed with locals, all wandering the covered market and most, like us, looking rather than buying.

At this time, both my wife and I agreed that we did not want to see another temple, so this morning's venture was a very welcome break from temples!

Although the shopping strips all seem to be the same narrow streets, being covered in most sections, to protect from the weather and many, many small shops selling anything and everything, with several selling the same thing!

Our welcome to Kochi. A wonderful musical team.

We did find a Daimaru Department Store, which was of interest and we noted that the pricing structure on known items was quite high in comparison to what we would pay at home, even allowing for a reasonable exchange rate.

We did venture down to the basement at this store to see a 'food hall' but this area was, like so many we had previously viewed, selling mostly sweet cakes and chocolates... of every description and not much else. You would be in your element if you were a, "chocoholic". We were beginning to wonder where the locals bought their meat, fruit and veg, plus of course, general household items. We did see a couple of small butchers' shops in the main shopping strips, but their range of meats often appeared to focus mainly on fairly fatty Wagu beef or fatty pork products and all quite expensive.

We also wondered why the Japanese, (in the main, small, slim people), weren't a great deal bigger with all of these styles of meats and those, many chocolate and sweet products being in abundance, which they seemed to love.

Leaving this Department Store we were lucky to find ourselves exiting right next to the Bus Stop of the ship's shuttle bus service and managed to get a seat straight away and we headed back to the port.

Arriving back at the port there were cars and coaches parked everywhere and once again, we could see a huge group of locals, all waving and smiling, with flags flying and a couple of groups playing violins and other stringed instruments. Mostly youngsters and very well trained in their particular instrument.

The crowd of locals again building in numbers towards the afternoon and our departure time and more flag waving and musical displays occurring, with certain groups joining the throng every few minutes it seemed.

It all appeared to be quite a genuine "thank-you" for visiting in their waving and was quite humbling to have all these 'well-wishers' waving you goodbye.

Return to Kobe

Following a smooth sailing night, the morning saw us arrive back in the port of Kobe, which was now quite familiar, with the surrounding buildings and sweeping elevated roadway located just beyond the main port building.

Once again, a large group of flag wavers and a local band were there to welcome us.

Nearly all the Japanese, who had joined us the week before were now dis-embarking, but a similar number were getting on.

We did have another tour booked for this stop, but we again made a cancellation, as this was to be a ten-hour tour and having already done one of similar time and venues, we decided to just catch the shuttle bus into the nearest shopping centre and once again have a walk around. I was still keen to find a supermarket, as I like to see what the locals eat and what the prices of goods are in general.

The shuttle bus dropped us and about fifty-five others at the entrance to the usual, 'market street'.

The bus only had seats for about thirty, but around an extra twenty-five of us were ushered on board also and just stood in the gangway, the driver more than happy to drive on. The seats themselves were fitted with 'compulsory' seat belts, so not quite sure of the legal position on those passengers standing.

It was only a short trip, about fifteen minutes, but I dread to think what might have happened if the driver suddenly had to break hard. I don't think the old lady standing next to the driver would have survived, with about a dozen of her fellow passengers at least, landing on top of her!

Anyway, once off the bus it was the usual market street, but as it wasn't quite ten in the morning, a lot of shops were still closed. Some not opening until 11.00am.

So, we wandered for a while and then decided to have a coffee, which turned out to be a very expensive coffee in a department store and following this we then ventured back onto the street. By now most of the shops were finally open for business and the street was quite crowded with people and presumably this was due to this Monday being still part of the Long-weekend holiday.

There were a few more 'up-market' shops here and again the prices of certain products, like shoes and clothing appeared reasonably expensive, although the quality looked good.

After a couple of hours of this we decided to stroll back to the shuttle bus stop and this just happened to be located right outside another Daimaru store. And as we approached, we could see a small queue waiting for the next bus. It was then that a couple we had met a few days earlier came out of the store and made us aware that there was a very good food hall downstairs, similar to their John Lewis store back home in England, where they were from.

"You must go and visit", they said.

So, we waved them goodbye and entered the main entrance and turned right and ventured down some concrete steps to this food hall.

Well, this food hall was possibly going to be the closest thing we would see that would resemble a supermarket that we would have at home. Quite a good range of fruit, vegetables and meat, all very well packaged and the usual 'supermarket goodies', plus the usual sugary sweet stuff; cakes, pastries and cookies and of course so many varieties of chocolates. Once again, the prices of the products were reasonably higher than we were used to back home.

We had a good 'sticky beak' at the various food sections and whilst there in front of us were the usual products that we would see in our own supermarkets, their wrapping and presentation was quite 'pretty' and precise.

Following a more in-depth look at what was on offer at this store, we then headed for the same stairwell and back up to the bus stop, just in time to jump on board a shuttle bus, as it was about to pull away. Fifteen minutes later we were back on board our 'steel home' and heading for our room, to get our hands washed and back out to the dining room for a late, but welcome lunch.

That evening on leaving the port, we were once again entertained by, the local entourage of bands, singers and flag wavers. They were there in force and wishing us all a safe onward journey and once more we sailed away, this time heading for China and the port city of Shanghai, which we would reach in two days-time.

Also, that evening there was a pleasant change to our usual format, with Geoff and Jane, an English couple that had befriended Dave and Linda, who we'd also chatted to a couple of times, inviting the four of us to, pre-dinner drinks in their cabin on the fifth level, right at the very back of the ship.

Geoff and Jane were in their early seventies, although acted like they were much younger. They were good conversationalists, although Geoff was a 'cricket tragic' and would tell us of his exploits at several grounds around the world. Before joining the ship in Sydney, he had the pleasure of attending a lunch at the MCG, in Melbourne. Geoff and Jane were in the Queen's Grill, the section of passengers just above us, we being in the Princess Grill level.

One of Geoff's reasons for the, drinks invitation, was that part of his 'room package', was "free beer and spirits", delivered to his room on a seemingly endless basis. This system was what we experienced on our last trip, previously described.

Geoff said that he and Jane couldn't possibly drink it all and would we like some bottles of gin, as he had much more than he could drink … although he did try. Of course, we were all happy to oblige and reduce his ever-increasing stock, so the 6.00pm invite was agreed.

It was a very pleasant 'Happy Hour' prior to dinner and we had a good go at reducing some of Geoff's drinks stock.

We were also given a quick tour of the outdoor section of their cabin, which was just a little more spacious than ours, but their cabin was more, square in shape, rather than the oblong of most. And wrapping around the square of their cabin this outdoor section was quite private.

The only downside of a cabin at the rear they said, was the rocking motion of the ship in rough seas...of which there had been a few of late!

Leaving Jane and Geoff's cabin, the six of us made our way to floor eleven and the Grills Restaurants for dinner. Geoff and Jane heading in the same direction, but turning right into the Queens restaurant, the four of us banking left, into the Princess Grill's restaurant.

Arriving at our table, we see already sat in her favourite chair, Margareta was back and was obviously pleased to have caught up with her son in Kobe and she very much enjoyed their time together. The table was now with the five of us, no one else to join us, to replace Joan.

A bit more space around the table, with Margareta regaining her favored spot, toward the top of the table, looking down the restaurant, somewhat like the Queen Bee.

Alex, our waiter providing a very wide smirk, as we joined the table, making a silent statement that, "she's back"!

Shanghai here we come.

We now had two days at sea, with the usual, drinks, eating and chit chat, with our fellow shipmates. On the Thursday morning around 7.00am, we arrived in the extremely busy port of Shanghai, situated in the very spacious section of the Huangpu River, with ships and boats of all sizes, seemingly everywhere.

Positioned on the coast of the East China Sea, Shanghai is China's largest city, with a population around 25 million...about as many as the whole of Australia!

Shanghai has a strong foreign influence, this being driven by the old trade route established through the East hundreds of years ago, but it grew rapidly following the first, Opium War in 1842, when the Chinese Government surrendered Shanghai to the British Government.

The city was then opened up to the rest of the world, led by the British, who were not subject to Chinese law.

Shortly after, the Americans and the French took an active interest and so began an influx of traders and bankers making Shanghai and its' port a very large commercial centre.

However, before we got up this morning a small 'tragedy' occurred.

We awoke at 6.30am and dozing around 6.40am, when there was this almighty WOOSH, followed immediately by a rather loud bang from the bathroom area.

I ventured slowly and tentatively into the bathroom, expecting to see it blown-up, but no, the only visible difference was no water in the bowl. I pressed the flush button, but nothing happened. Hmmm, what now?

While contemplating our next move, there was an even louder WOOSH/BANG, actually more of a BOOM. Crikey, I thought, what the hell was that. I ventured timidly back into the bathroom, definitely expecting to see through the wall to the corridor outside, but no, the only difference was, there now was water in the toilet bowl.

Hmmm, I leant forward … I didn't have a very good track record with toilets of late … but I once again pushed the flush button... nothing, not even a gurgle, the water sat there, a little grey I thought.

So … I put on my shorts and opened our front door half expecting a corridor of fellow passengers wanting to know, "what the hell was that"? But nothing, I was the only one out there, surely this major 'catastrophe' can't just be our problem, I thought. My wife was still in bed muttering something about, "I think I need to go to the happy room". I said you'd better put on your clothes as I think you'll have to go to the happy room upstairs.

At that moment, still not 7.00 am yet, our room Steward, Pat appeared, announcing a major problem and "people were onto it... but best to go upstairs and across to the Starboard side", as this Port side, all the way along was, in his words, "Kaput"!

Both myself and my wife, disappeared upstairs to the Commodore Club area to search out a working loo, luckily no one else there... yet.

Returning downstairs to our cabin we still had no toilet, but we did have running water, so could at least shower and wash ourselves.

My wife was getting breakfast delivered that morning (the first time ever), as she was headed out on an early coach tour, of around four hours, hopefully back for lunch ... Ha Ha.

This particular tour she was going on was ultimately heading for the 'Bullet Train' station, where she would experience a super-fast trip out to the airport, at around 450 KPH.

A journey of normally 45 minutes by car, suddenly reduced to around 7 minutes by this 'magnetic rail ', although there was no rail as such, just a magnetic field, hovering… Hmmm!

Shit! I exclaimed, I was staying on board, I valued my life and anyway, we've been to Shanghai before and spent four days here and I didn't need to get off today... I was writing my first book… much safer in my opinion. After all, this was the China Bullet train, not the Japanese one. The Japanese have been doing this stuff for years... China...Hmmm!

With my wife heading out for the morning, I got ready to have breakfast in the, "get-out-of-my-way buffet".

Shaving and doing my teeth there was suddenly another, WHOOSH/BOOM, it was the toilet, coming back on stream, if you'll excuse the expression. It was 9.15am.

Two and a half hours later than that first BOOM… All systems Go!

One of the reasons I didn't go on the trip with my wife was that, originally when making the booking (from home), you were supposed to have a visa for China, some on board, especially the Americans had paid hundreds of dollars to get a Visa. I couldn't be bothered, especially as we'd been to Shanghai only a few years before. So, I declined.

Then Cunard announced that if you were on a coach tour, you didn't require a Visa.... a bloody good job my wife had not gotten around to gaining it.

But by the time this information reached us I couldn't be bothered and while the fast train would have been an experience, this was China!!

And then, on the day prior to arriving in port, the Chinese apparently changed tack completely, stating if you carry a photocopy of the first, Photo page of your passport, with a Chinese Bar-Code stamped in it, you could go anywhere and you didn't need a Visa. Hmmm… there were a number of travelers totally pissed off, some as I mentioned, spending hundreds of dollars to buy their Visas prior to going on board.

Another stuff-up and not sure who to blame! But Cunard on-board staff came up with the approved photocopy of the passport, including the approved barcode, 24 hours before they were required. There are over 2000 of us on board...Hmmm!

Lunchtime came and my wife's scheduled time back was 1.00pm, but she didn't return until 2.30pm. She rang me to tell me the trip was running late, so I went to the buffet and ate a small Asian dish, which repeated on me for the rest of the day!

I no longer eat peppers, or specifically, Capsicums and the range of meals in the buffet appear to have peppers in everything (bar the desserts), with big and small bits of Capsicum. And even if I pick it out, the taste still lingers in the respective dish. Must be old age, as I used to love peppers, but no longer.

My wife returned from her very fast trip, starving, so the buffet was the first stop after a trip to the, now working, loo.

Is it my imagination, or does her facial skin look drawn backwards... 450kph was it?

In the Grill's bar that evening, prior to dinner, Geoff and Jane are already finishing their pre-dinner drinks and about to head to dinner, hoping to be out in time for a particular show in the Theatre. Geoff hasn't been too good of late, getting the "Cunard Cough" and runny nose.

Some fellow travelers put this down to the room air conditioning system, which dries the air and obviously the body fluids. Although Geoff was definitely keeping up his 'body fluids', Chardonnay I think his favorite is. He believes this ' medicine' is working and feels a lot better than he did! And I must agree, he did have a bit of a spring in his step!

I also have had this cough, which I have decided is better described as, 'kennel cough'... it has a ring to it. We once had a dog that got kennel cough when we placed her at kennels, when we were away for a long weekend. Thankfully she was not too bad and resumed normal health quite quickly.

I also resumed normal health quite quickly, but I think this was mostly due to my medicinal brandy each evening!

The following day Friday, we had been given 'free' tickets to a wine tasting in the afternoon, being held in the larger restaurant of the Britannia room, with a 3.00pm start.

This was, 'free', because on this cruise my wife and I reached Platinum Level, having travelled on Cunard ships with a total of over seventy days. This was over a period of nine years, so wasn't instant. This level also had certain other benefits too … we could get our laundry done by the staff and now get a twenty percent discount on the price... Gosh how lucky are we!

No more maneuvers for the public laundry... that would be worth paying 80 percent for!

Well, the wine tasting was, 'vin ordinaire' and we were so glad we didn't have to pay for that! Only four wines, mostly the cheap end from Chile or one of their South American cousins, unfortunately, not their good stuff (of which there are plenty of examples).

In this tasting they even had a Gewurtztraminer. Now I thought this wine was only from Alsace and leaning towards German origin but no, someone called, Pablo Morande' from south of Santiago had produced this one. To be fair it wasn't too bad and definitely the best of the four 'suspects'. Ah well, back to the good old Penfolds Bin 28 for dinner. … Honkers here we come.

We were looking forward to Hong Kong, our final port, as we were leaving the ship at this point. We had been to "Honkers" a couple of times before. The last time we were there my cousin, who had lived there for around twenty-five years at that stage, had shown us parts of the surrounding country that we hadn't seen before and in particular we were taken to a coastal area where fish were straight off the trawlers and a local on-site restaurant, provided us with a great treat.

However, this time to H.K. my cousin, in her wisdom, had retired and moved to Turkey, yes Turkey.

So, this trip without my cousin's local knowledge, we were planning only a couple of tourist staples. The usual walking the streets and window shopping and a, much anticipated ride on the fast ferry to Macau.

We also had a dinner booked at a three Michelin Star Chinese Restaurant called T'ang Court, situated in the hotel Langham, where we were booked to stay.

However, this day it all went, 'pear-shaped'!!

On the Sunday we left the ship... luggage gathered, we awaited our previously booked, 'Van-Limo' to pick us up from the wharf-side waiting area, right on the harbour side, next to the Queen Elizabeth.

The 'Van-limo' eventually arrived, we loaded up and headed out of the port area... three minutes later we were being dropped off at The Langham. The hotel was literally just around the corner... a $90 trip thank you very much. We could have walked if we had known, although struggling with three large suitcases, by now weighing the proverbial ton, plus our hand luggage and our duty-free bags... not a good look to arrive sweating at a Five Star Hotel!

I said previously this is where it went "pear-shaped". The previous Saturday evening, returning to our cabin following dinner … and a nightcap, I wasn't too good, rushing to the Happy Room (as we had now permanently christened it).

So, on this Sunday morning my tummy still wasn't the best.

After booking in at the hotel's reception, we headed for our allocated room and took the lift to the fourth floor...

In the lift there was a notice affixed to the side-wall panel, with a fairly gloomy message, it read … "When there is a fire, do not use the lift"

So, I was thinking … when is the next fire?

Settling into our very comfortable hotel room (thank goodness it was ready at 10.30am) I spent that Sunday and most of the next four days either in bed or in the 'Happy Room'.

Oh wonderful... Noro-Virus. Yes, this was Noro-Virus … not Covid Virus!!

I had caught Noro-Virus once before on a small cruise we had done a few years before, so I knew what I had. This illness can sometimes be found on cruise ships, due to living with a large number of guests and once the illness is in the circle, it can spread quite easily.

You take all the precautions on board, wash your hands a thousand times a day, squirt that antiseptic blue stuff on your hands before entering the buffet and avoid anyone who, coughs, sneezes or generally doesn't look well and ... I obviously slipped up somewhere. Self-service food buffets are probably the leading offender in being the catalyst to spread the germ... handling service tongs and other products, such as salt & pepper pots, prime examples.

We are definitely hoping that buffet service will be replaced in future.

So, me being unwell meant we didn't get to Macau or ride the famous Hong Kong ferry around the waterway or partake of wonderful food in the three Michelin Star Cantonese Restaurant. (Although given the price of our two coffees in the foyer cafe area of the hotel, costing around A$23.50, I think missing out on this dinner was possibly the best result for my wallet)!

No, excitement was definitely off the menu. On the Tuesday I did manage to drag myself down Peking Road to the eleventh floor of a building housing several Doctors and although a very busy surgery waiting room greeted us, I got instant attention from an English doctor, or maybe he was Irish, a Doctor Francis Martin O'Tremba. He'd been a resident of Honkers for forty years he told me.

I struggled back to the hotel with a box of Penicillin tablets, a packet of Lomotil pills and three bottles of, what turned out to be, a disgusting tasting, sickly sweet white liquid, which according to the label I was to have; four tea spoons of five mils. every four hours??

Now I think something got lost in translation here. Surely, I thought, I could take one, twenty mil. spoonful every four hours, who would know. But then I realized that this should have read, one five mil. spoonful every four hours! However, after the first ten mils. I gave up on this horrible white goo, not consuming anymore and placed all the bottles in the waste bin upon booking out of the hotel.

Thankfully I was considerably improved on the day we flew out of Hong Kong on the very pleasant Qantas night flight back to Brisbane, arriving in the early hours.

Travel... not only does it open your mind and eyes!

Our Entry to Busan Port, South Korea

Call me a "Glutton for Punishment", but our next cruise is already booked and I am looking forward to this next cruise, coming up soon.

The "Bullet Train" — Shanghai.

The Local Cruise

We are booked onto a shipping line not experienced before, (but the one I made mention of previously), Holland America's, "The Nordam." ...We live in anticipation!

This cruise will also cover a similar course as our first mention at the start of this book. Although we are sailing from Sydney this time, then down to Melbourne and on to Tassie and then across to New Zealand. So, I will not bore you with similar tales, but highlight differences, which I trust will be both insightful and provide a few smiles!

These style of short cruises around our region, not only allow us locals to enjoy a relaxing holiday, but they also try to provide the first-time cruiser with a cost-effective trip which of course, will 'hook' you into doing many future longer cruises... which was certainly the case with ourselves some years' ago. But that's another story!

Sydney again...Park Hyatt again ...Cruising again.

The Park Hyatt is once again its' usual friendly, welcoming self and our room (an upgrade we are informed), overlooks the Harbour and this time has views of the famous Opera House, with the famous Bridge, to our back.

We're only here for one day in Sydney, before jumping on this new ship for us and although we will venture over similar territory, it's territory that we love.

This ship is very similar in size and layout to the Queen Elizabeth, which is not a total surprise as Holland America is owned by Carnival, the same owner as the Queen Elizabeth. (Through the Cunard Group).

After settling into the hotel, we head off for a good walk around the Rocks area, window shopping as usual before stopping at The Coffee house, in the Rocks section of shops. We're to enjoy a coffee and a shared...chocolate cake, before heading back to our room to relax, before getting ready for dinner.

Our dinner table has been booked for at least a couple of months prior to our trip, as we our splashing out this time and heading for the Bennelong Restaurant at the Opera House. After about eighteen months being closed, the restaurant is now in the very capable hands of Chef Peter Gilmore, the chef/part owner of Quay Restaurant, just across the water at the end of the Large Cruise Terminal. This is where a number of cruise ships commence their journey out of Sydney. (Although not for us this trip, as our cruise starts from White Bay, a twenty-minute taxi ride away, on the other side of the Harbour).

I am reasonably familiar with the Bennelong Restaurant, as I have had the pleasure of being there a few times over the years, although not always dining, mostly through business.

Two companies that I have been associated with over the years, having been contracted to manage the food outlets of this site.

However, I can never forget my very first time at this famous location which was about 41 years' ago when I first arrived in Australia. Prior to leaving the U.K. and emigrating here, I had approached two companies for possible employment.

One of those companies was a contract caterer, who amongst their various contracts at that time was the Opera House and they managed the food service outlets on site, including the fine dining restaurant of The Bennelong. I was invited to attend an interview with this organisation and this iconic location was designated the venue to be interviewed, meeting with the then General Manager, Brien Trippas.

Attending an interview for a new job is a little nerve racking at the best of times, but being in a new country and situated in one of the world's most iconic buildings, on Sydney Harbour, overlooking another iconic structure, The Bridge … is something else.

However, my 'interrogator' was very welcoming and relaxed, shaking my hand and saying; "call me Brien" and "would you like a beer", well it was late afternoon and I of course replied in the affirmative!

This was my introduction to business in Australia, sat in the Bennelong Restaurant, of the very famous Opera House, having a beer...how great was that!

I was employed and so commenced my Australian working life and although my position with the company was actually based in Melbourne, over the years I attended a few times at the Opera House, mostly in a work capacity. However, I am always reminded of my very first encounter here, when I'm in Sydney.

Anyway, our dinner at this very special venue that evening was excellent, although a tad expensive, but hey, you don't do this every day of the week!

The following morning after breakfast and a bit of a chat with the Maitre' d as encountered on our earlier visit, we packed our cases, paid our account, hailed a cab and headed off in the direction of White Bay. Arriving twenty minutes later and gaining instant access to our ship's cabin, ... following the usual security arrangements.

Once on board it was again obvious that the staff are mostly from the Philippines, with their usual friendly smiles and welcomes, but you already know that some will not always be the best trained in their roles. Though friendliness always overcomes any shortcomings in service.

We soon discover that the food on board is O.K., but nothing to, "write home about". This understanding was therefore an incentive to explore alternative dining options, when in the various ports of call.

The ship's wine selection is basic and certainly drinkable, but mostly unknown brands, from the States, with just a couple of 'Aussies' thrown in, mostly of the cheaper variety, but not priced this way on the ship's wine list! ...And again, when you come to pay your ship's bill, it is in American Dollars. So, an amount as much as an extra 35% can be added to the wine menu listing, due to our Exchange Rate...That's Life!

Still, our cabin is larger than on the QE and does have a separate bath in the ensuite, so not all bad and the price of this 14-day cruise over to New Zealand, visiting several ports on both islands, is acceptable.

Although on our way to New Zealand, the ship heads firstly to Melbourne, where we had previously arranged to catch up with our long-term Accountants. It's, 'that time of year' and we're taking with us a heavy carry bag, full of our annual Tax paperwork for them to work their 'magic', prior to the usual scrutiny of the ATO.

This pre-arranged meeting with Con, our accountant contact was opportune, as we had prior to leaving home, been searching for a new home and discussions hadn't gone our way. However, during the first few hours on board the ship, things had changed and negotiations had re-commenced. But reading paperwork and signing pages was not that simple on-board ship, so catching up with our accountant enabled us to print things off and 'sign our lives away' and get the necessary paperwork trail started, on our way to owning a new, well… renovated pad!

We were in Melbourne until 11.30pm that evening and this allowed us to venture out to dinner to a restaurant on-shore. So, we caught a taxi to Sails Restaurant in Elwood, right on the beach, about a twenty-minute taxi ride from our berth at Station Pier. We had been to this restaurant only once before, so we were hoping our trip this time would again provide a wonderful dinner.

And yes, it was excellent, together with a delightful wine and then we returned to the ship, ready to set sail down to Hobart, the next port of call.

As previously noted, we have been to Hobart many times before and it is a favourite of ours, together with Tasmania generally. We enjoy its' food scene, both in the capital and surrounding suburbs. We've also ventured down the coast to regions such as Bruny Island and visited all of this island's various food focussed businesses, such as Oysters, Cheeses and Chocolates!

Well... pulling into dock at the Main Pier, things looked a little quiet for a work day in Hobart city…

Guess What! It's ... Show Day in Hobart... a Public Holiday! Most shops and eateries closed and if it is open, the cafes and restaurants that is, there is a, "Surcharge of 10%"!

Well this day we didn't venture too far, strolling across the internal section of the Harbour's moving bridge. A short stroll from here we pass our favourite, the famous and very delightful and iconic, Mures Fish Building.

Here they have a collection of eateries, with their Restaurant located upstairs and downstairs, on the ground level, a Fresh Fish section ... with yummy Crayfish as usual, plus their Café, etc. Moving on past Mures, it was then on up into Salamanca Place for a, "look see" only buying a newspaper and once again a Lotto ticket... just in case I get lucky and win, "the big one"! And no, I didn't, again!!

We ventured back across the small park towards the dock and spotted the building where the restaurant, 'Aloft' is situated and strode in, in the hope of booking for dinner, as we were to be in Hobart 'till late that evening. However, like a lot of other local eateries, being a, Public-holiday they were closed all day.

However, not all was lost, the restaurant/bar directly beneath the 'Aloft' restaurant, 'The Glass House', in the same building was open, so, we ventured in and booked for a 6.30pm dinner.

The exterior of the MACq 01 Hotel, at the Hobart Dock

Coles Freycinet Bay

We had a chat and joke with the chef who was busy in the kitchen preparing food and then moved on, back across the moving bridge towards the ship.

The Glass House was an apt name for the restaurant, being housed in a building with vast glass windows.

On our way back to our floating home, we passed the new hotel, MACq 01, recently opened, virtually right next to the ship on Macquarie Wharf. So, we walked in to check it out, as we would be staying in this new hotel in a few months' time in mid-January, when we return to Tassie on a holiday break in the New Year.

The hotel had a very friendly bunch of staff that welcomed us in to have a closer look. We were shown a couple of different hotel suites and also given a brief walk around the restaurant and bar sectors, closed at the time we were there. The hotel was in a very convenient location, being right on the dockside and close to a number of good restaurants and only a short walk to the city centre.

A very busy Hobart Port on the day we leave

Since this time, my wife and I have stayed at this hotel each time we have been in Hobart. We recommend it to all our friends when they are travelling this way.

Leaving port that evening was a smooth sail-away, but quite soon we were out in the open sea and a little more, 'choppy', beginning our trek across "The Ditch", to New Zealand.

PRINCESS CRUISES

No, this was not us leaving Hobart! Parliament House had held a meeting this day and this was the Governor being escorted home.

New Zealand

After a couple of relaxing sea days, we arrived in the waters of Milford Sound, just for an easy, relaxed sail around this large water fjord and view the surrounding high hills and mountains in this beautiful spot. It was then on to Dunedin for the start of the New Zealand selection of ports.

However, the following morning when we arrived, it was into an early morning blanket of FOG!

This fog was so dense that you could not see further than about a metre in front of you and therefore the ship was unable to enter the port itself.

It wasn't until about noon that the ship finally docked, well overdue and the captain decided that due to this current cool weather pattern the ship would leave early at around 4.00 p.m., instead of 6.00pm, in an endeavour to miss the afternoon fog!

Well, 'best laid plans' and all that, the weather gods didn't like this, so at 3.00 pm the heavy fog fell over us again and so the decision was taken to stay overnight and leave around midday tomorrow.

Dunedin is located towards the lower part of the South Island and we have been before, having driven around the island a few years earlier.

With much less time in the region, due to the very late docking of the ship, we were somewhat restricted on our outing to the city. A little 'window shopping' and a cup of coffee was pretty much it, with a taxi ride there and back.

The most memorable thing of that day was, as previously mentioned, on leaving the city on our return to the port. Our taxi left via a main road from the retail sector and we entered a right turn lane with the appropriate arrow painted on the road (one of two right turn lanes). However, following the painted arrow, also painted on the road were the words; LEFT TURN ONLY. Our taxi driver was as amused as us, stating that, “council sometimes gets it wrong”!

NEXT PORT ---- PICTON

We had no difficulty pulling into the port this time, no fog, probably due to Picton being at the top end, slightly warmer end, of the South Island.

Again, we have been to this part of the South Island a few times over the past few years.

Once off the ship we walked through the very pretty and quite green open park area, with the odd palm tree swaying in the light breeze. Leaving this lovely park, we walk across to the retail section.

As is often the rule for my wife and I, especially escaping the ship early, we search out a café to enjoy a good cup of coffee. New Zealand has always amazed us in the provision of a quality cuppa, even in the remotest of towns and villages.

Coming from Melbourne originally, where coffee is…’special’, a quality coffee is sometimes harder to find, and often our palate is aggrieved, when judged against our old stomping grounds.

However, we have always been impressed by our New Zealand offerings.

I personally also believe these days, with so many individual roasting companies in the market place, that the offering gets ‘clouded’ and therefore too individual!

And when you only drink, Long Black (with no milk) as I do, you can identify a poor roast much more easily.

Anyway, having enjoyed a good cuppa, we moved off to once again window shop and see what’s on offer…maybe a bargain or two!

Although when a large cruise liner is in port, the retailers have excellent talent at encouraging the passengers to, “Come inside and check us out”!

We did have a good walk around the shops and got a bit of welcome exercise along the way and of course, checked out the many food houses, for somewhere for lunch.

Our choice for lunch was a little restaurant, quite full (always a good sign) and a simple, not long menu, with a few fish dishes. Our eating habits these days include two or three days a week eating fish of some variety and the fish available in N.Z. is always good, Mahi-Mahi being a favourite.

Following a good lunch and before we ventured back to our 'steel home', we retraced our steps back to the park and enjoyed some musicians playing guitars and singing, who had set up near the entrance. The ship was berthed not far away, so we stayed a while to hear some excellent renditions of some 'familiar oldies'

Our next stop tomorrow is Wellington, which is situated at the base of the North Island, Wellington being the official capital of New Zealand.

WELLINGTON

The city of Wellington is nicknamed, "The Windy City", due to the often, strong winds, blowing through the Cook Strait.

It has a population of around half a million residents, making it the second most populated city in N.Z. and located where it is on the … Fault Line, is known for both its' windy days and earth tremors!

Having been to Wellington a couple of times, as previously mentioned earlier, by the time we reach this city this time we have, "been there and done that". However, it's an easy city to relax in and this day all we seemed to do was window shop and have a coffee in one of its' many cafés. Still, it's an enjoyable place to visit and unwind.

NAPIER

The following day we are in Napier for a one-day stop. This day was mostly about visiting a couple of local wineries in the Hawkes Bay region and Napier is central to.

Mission Estate and Brookfields Wineries were selected and an enjoyable tour and talk on wines was held at both.

Mission Estate is situated in a very elegantly restored Seminary building in the Taradale Hills. The area it sits on has sweeping views across the vineyards and the coast beyond. It is listed as the oldest winery in New Zealand, established in 1851, by French Missionaries and today produces a wide selection of both red and white varietals.

Brookfields Vineyards founded in 1937, is considered to be Hawke's Bay's, "Oldest Boutique" winery and produces around 12,000 to 14,000 cases of wine each year, from a selection of localised vineyards in Hawkes Bay. It is situated near to the Tutaekuri River, between Hastings and Napier.

Both these wineries are well worth a visit if you are visiting this region.

TAURANGA

The following day we arrived in the city of Tauranga and were quickly tied up at the dock (the ship, not us), quite close to the city centre.

Again, we have been to Tauranga a few times and find the area a very easy place to get around and have enjoyed staying a few days on each of our visits on our previous travels to the area by road.

This particular day, a Saturday, my wife had decided to take one of the ship's half-day tours to nearby Rotorua, noted for its' Hot Pools, including the "Bubbling Hot, Mud Pools".

We had both been to Rotorua a few years' before, so I decided I would stay local and do a little walking and relax with a bit of window shopping as well.

I was also writing my first book during this period, so I was using some of this, 'Me-Time' and busy at the i-pad!

So, waving my wife's coach Bon Voyage, in the early part of the morning, I set off on my walk along the beachfront, which flowed on from the port.

Now I have to advise here that I have the number 28 as one of my lucky numbers. Over the years my wife and I, as we have moved around the country, have actually owned 4 homes with that as our street number...purely coincidental, definitely unplanned.

In addition to this, a few significant happenings in our lives have occurred on the 28th day. I came to Australia when I was

28 and my first employment here, commenced on the 28th of September and just over three years later our first business was officially commenced, on the 28th of January.

So, this day on my walk along the beachfront I pass a very large, handsome looking house… No. 28, a rather large two storey mansion style, in its' own manicured grounds. Situated of course, right across from the beach, very nice!

I walked on turning left into a side street and I see myself passing a property; actually, a Duplex, No.28 A and No.28 B. Very nice properties on the one large block, with quite modern sharp features and I am a little bemused that I keep seeing the No.28.

Well on I go and then I have to take a left turn to head towards the main shopping centre. A little way along this street, "blow me down with a feather", I find myself passing yet another house with the number 28 on its' gatepost…I give a little smile.

Now here is the weird bit…as I turn into the main shopping strip and walk a few metres, I can see along the pavement an 'A' Board outside a newsagent's shop…the Headline shouts at me; "$28 million in tonight's Lotto Draw"!

Well, this is too much of a coincidence, are 'forces from beyond' (whatever that means!), trying to tell me something? … I must of course make entry into the shop and buy a ticket in this night's Lotto Draw. 28 million hey!

I venture in and 'lash out'… I buy a $10 ticket.

That ticket unfortunately did not win the "Big One"

However, I did have a win... (and I kid you not!) … my win was $28 Dollars!!

So, Tauranga has a special place in my memory.

It must also be noted here that Tauranga is classified as a city and very much linked to the coastal section of, Mount Maunganui, a short walking distance away, which is classified I believe, as a suburb of Tauranga.

Together on this coastal peninsula, they form a very pleasant region along this Eastern side of the North Island and well worth staying a few days, if you are heading to N.Z.

This region has a few good beaches for swimming and also sections where boating activity takes place and is also where you can throw in a fishing line, for some worthwhile catches.

Cafes and restaurants are good and again, a cup of coffee is always a treat.

The shopping strip is also worth a wander and my wife has always found a "bargain" in the "ladies" shops, which are very well represented in this sector.

Oh… I did buy a shirt here once!

AUCKLAND

The following day we arrived at our final cruising destination, Auckland.

We will be dis-embarking here and staying for a few days at our favourite hotel.

Once again in Auckland, our final destination on this cruise and here we are tied up right alongside the Hilton Hotel, in the dock area. This location is very nearly right in the city centre, well the edge, but still fairly central to everything.

However, we are not staying at this hotel.

Auckland is a city we know quite well, having visited about a dozen times previously. So, leaving the ship that day we headed the short distance (via taxi) along the waterfront and around to the area known as, The Viaduct.

Situated in a very pleasant part of this waterfront position is our hotel, The Sofitel, a hotel that we have stayed at most of the times that we have found ourselves in Auckland. This stay we will be here for four days, before flying home.

The hotel is low rise and holds a quality in both its' staff and services and has both an on-site restaurant and café, that are hard to beat. Plus, the rooms come with a balcony attached and windows that can be opened, which is very much my preference these days. High-rise hotels, with non-opening windows are not for me and I am reminded of a conversation held on a radio station in Melbourne, a few years' ago. A local fire inspector was being interviewed regarding a recent, 'high-rise' fire and this inspector stated that, if you were situated higher than the 13th floor, the fire service would not be able to reach you, if there was a fire!

So, low rise is definitely the Go!

From our hotel it's an easy walk into the city or slightly further up the hill, to the feature of this city, the very distinguished, Sky Tower… they have very good firework displays!!

This is a telecommunication/broadcasting tower, of some 328 mtrs. high and the tallest building in the Southern Hemisphere, which strikes an imposing face to the city and suburbs beyond.

Well worth a trip to the top, or at least to the section the public can ascend to and see the majestic view over the City and Harbours.

We like to hire a car here and this gives a little more flexibility to travel to nearby areas, such as St. Heliers beach or Devonport or to one of a range of pleasant suburbs. Although we do enjoy the very quick ferry trip across to the town of Devonport and in most of these suburbs, you'll find a few good restaurants and cafés.

I have previously talked about this region earlier, so will move on, but travelling our region, of OZ and N.Z. on a cruise ship is well worth the money. It is both relaxing as well as informative, even if you have been before, as my wife and I have. We still love our trips in this region and know we will always discover different things

The port of Auckland, Waitemata Harbour.

New Holiday – Cruise and Tour

Well, here is a special memory… we have arrived at the 'real' start of our Alaskan/Canadian soirée. We have flown from the Sunshine Coast, across to Auckland, with a one-night stopover. Early the following morning, we are up and heading to Auckland's International Airport, catching a flight with Air New Zealand over to San Francisco.

Here, in San Fran, we are on another, one-night stopover and staying at a hotel we know well, up on Knob Hill, The Ritz Carlton… Great hotel, friendly staff, good eateries and a very relaxing environment. We will return… The next day it's back to the airport, as we are to fly on up to Anchorage for a couple of days acclimatizing.

It is here that we are readying ourselves for the trip that will be very new to us, starting on the cruise ship, Celebrity Millennium and sailing to many ports on the Alaskan coast.

The full two days (three nights) that are spent at the Hilton Embassy Suites in Anchorage are relaxing and although the accommodation is more in keeping with a large motel, it is very welcoming and "homely". There are also other benefits, like the "Happy Hour" each day, actually a two-hour period from 5.30pm through to 7.30pm, when the bar is open and you can get two free drinks each, prior to heading to the dining room for a reasonable dinner and an inexpensive bottle of red!

This is our first trip to Alaska and Canada and we are looking forward to seeing everything, from Bears to Glaciers and our starting point is Anchorage.

This city is basically at the very end of this American peninsula and on certain high vantage points, Russian territory can be viewed over the adjoining strip of water, The Bering-Straights.

It is interesting to me that this large section of land is part of America, rather than the adjoining country of Canada. However, it was originally part of Russia at the time it was "acquired" and at that stage Canada was a "Province" of Britain and not the best of mates with Russia, (America also at that time, not huge friends with Britain).

Alaska was purchased from the Russians in around 1867, for the then vast sum of approximately 7 million Dollars or .02c per acre, by the then American Government headed by President Lincoln and the purchase negotiations were led by the Secretary of State of that government, William Seward.

A lot of people at that time were questioning this "Deal", some suggesting that the American Government had purchased a, "Large Lump of Ice"! Today of course, with the continuing mining of coal, oil and even gold, still from regions such as The Yukon, makes Mr Seward look like a Genius!

Indeed, one museum notice indicated that the oil reserves, which commenced flowing in about 1977, were potentially 900 billion drums. Some lump of ice!

William Seward has a town named after him, which is situated south from Anchorage, about 150 miles away on the coast. It is here that our ship will board the passengers for the week-long cruise to Vancouver, sailing through the magnificent waters of the Gulf of Alaska or the Bering Sea.

We will be passing Glaciers with their huge lumps of ice floating by us, having broken away from these massive frozen waterways of some thousands of years old and this together with seemingly never-ending high mountain peaks, most covered in snow, make for absolutely spectacular viewing. The main glacier viewing will be Hubbard, entered from Yakutat Bay.

The day that we joined the ship had been planned, very carefully by the Celebrity cruise line. It commenced with most of the passengers (staying in Anchorage hotels) attending the Egan Hall in downtown Anchorage.

Signing in and completing all the necessary paperwork and loading their luggage onto a large truck, which set off before us to Seward for transfer to the ship.

We meantime were all loaded into a couple of coaches and transferred to the railway station to board the train, specifically engaged by Celebrity, to take us south to Seward, on a very slow train ride through the dramatic countryside of mountains, rivers and …GRIZZLY BEARS!

This train journey was a slow, four-hour plus trip, which was delightful, although a tad boring toward the end, having viewed all of the most amazing scenery in the first couple of hours or so, including that of a rather large black bear running across the rail line behind us, as we rounded a bend in the track.

Now you will recall that I sometimes mention incidences regarding "restrooms"…. On our Japanese venture the term, "Happy Rooms" was created by our tour guide and this nickname seemed appropriate at that time...that was until I had that misfortune with the water hose protruding from the toilet bowl in South Korea!

Now on our local tour of Anchorage, the term for 'Happy Rooms' has somewhat changed to, 'The Brown Shack' ... this is not what you're thinking...stop that...it is because the restrooms are mostly timber weather-board built units and all painted brown! The local tourist authority obviously liking the colour brown!

Well, on the morning of our departure from Anchorage, at the aforementioned Egan Hall, I thought a quick trip to the "Brown Shack Happy Room" was appropriate, considering our proposed, four and a half hours journey.

Entering this Restroom it appeared empty, however, from one of the many cubicles along the room I could hear this rather strong grumbling snore.

Fearing it might have been a Grizzly who had slept the night there, I tentatively had a closer look.

Well, my fear morphed into a big smile upon seeing a man's well-shod feet and attached ankles under the door. He was obviously a very tired traveller who had fallen fast asleep as… "nature had called".

Leaving him to snore I ventured back to the main room and informed security, (just in case he missed the train). The big guys with the side arms said they would check it out.

Thereafter of course, I couldn›t help but check out every set of shoes walking past to see who was this tired shipmate. Alas, he was not seen again!

Arriving in Seward late afternoon it was an easy transfer to our cruise ship and we settled in for a journey to the Glacier region of Hubbard, which we would arrive at early the next day.

On board that first evening was the usual, wining and dining and meeting a few of your fellow travel mates. This time though we were to be seated at a table for two only, so no 'table-mates' to chat to like we would usually do.

Up early for breakfast, our view outside was of; white hills, white mountains and white 'floating stuff'… Very large sections of ice broken away from the Glacier sectors, just floating past us … thankfully not too close!

This was the entry into the Hubbard Glacier sector and was an amazing picture, especially to us, sub-tropical folk.

It was a slow sail through this region and the surrounding flow of water and these large ice blocks were photographic material constantly. Plus, the occasional quite large Eagle flying over, heading to a few trees on land, also not far away.

Sunday, the 29th of July (Monday 30th in Australia), we arrived in Juneau. It only has a population of around 30,000, but is the Capital city of Alaska. (Anchorage has a population of around 300,000) ... Duh?

Apparently there is no road out of this town... only boat or flying boat appears to be the transport that will relocate you to other parts of the state etc.

Well Juneau was O.K., but not too exciting and once you've seen one jewellery shop and the one local souvenir shop... you've seen them all!

AND … these style of retail outlets, are everywhere.

So, the only other trip, as promoted heavily by our very friendly and jovial concierge, Josue', in the Michael's Club Bar on-board, is to lunch at Tracy's King Crab Shack, just off the port side, where we are docked. He eats lunch there every time the ship is in this port.

Yes, that's me having just eaten at Tracy's King Crab Shack. A long walk is now definitely required!

This place is busy, busy, busy, when we front up for lunch and Josue' is just leaving, having ventured there early, still officially on duty but with house-phone in hand, just in case he is required back on board.

Our chosen meal was a set meal for one, lots of crab legs, but quite ample for the two of us, American portions are quite large... much like a lot of them!

Following lunch it's back on board and an afternoon "Nanna-Nap" before preparation of our bodies for dinner. Another day over...

Monday (Tuesday back home), we're in Skagway, a medium sized town of around 2500, although this increases significantly in the summer months, with both "local" tourists and the many cruise ships, sailing in, which equate to 4 this day, boosting the town's numbers by as much ten thousand.

Today we're up early, 6.00am, as we are booked on a trip up into the mountains on a train, which turns out to be very basic selection of carriages, looking a bit sad.

Yes, looking at this train you wonder whether it'll make it all the way to the top, to an area in British Columbia Canada, called Fraser, although our American hosts keep calling it Frazier, not sure why. Maybe they get confused and associate the name pronunciation with the T.V. comedy, Frazier.

The train journey is about an hour and a half up, what can only be described as, the mountain side...literally. And we're sitting on the side of the train where, when you look out of the window, there is NOTHING, a shear drop, of hundreds of feet. A few pine trees are scattered in some sections but if the train suddenly, 'jumped the line', nothing would stop us falling all the way to the bottom of the valley below. The rail track clearing itself being no bigger than the train in most areas, hewn out of the mountain-side by the Gold-Rush miners of the early part of last Century!

One particular bridge we crossed over, was built in 1899 of timber and large iron bolts and passing over this historic bridge we can see absolutely "zero" below us. NOTHING was to be seen in the vast distance below. But this bridge is still in, we are told, "very good condition"! I shut my eyes at this point.

The prospectors of the early 1900's took months to get to their gold destination, mostly walking or if lucky, using horses. They had to carry with them months-worth of food stuffs as well as their other equipment and many did not make it. And even the ones that did manage to get to the Yukon region, arrived often a year later than the first discoveries were made, so very few made gold finds.

The building of the rail line, mostly along old tracks on the mountainside took a few years and involved truck-loads of explosives apparently, but creating the slim track on the very outer side of the mountains was a tremendous feat.

Today in that carriage we were in, there were vast sectors of NOTHING on our side and instant death if the train were to fall off the track!

The solid mountain on the other side of the carriage only had to crumble a little (as had happened only last year, thankfully without a train running by) and it would be, 'Goodnight Vienna'!

The most nerve-racking moments were when certain "photo opportunities" presented themselves and the passengers, sat on the mountain side of the train, all jumped up to take a photo, moving to our side of the train and obviously "adjusting" the weight distribution!! My eyes were often shut!

Thankfully we did reach the summit with no issues and to return home to our starting point, we switched transport with another group, who were on the way back down from the mountains. We were transported by an awaiting coach, on the only highway through this section. The other group now taking our place and returning to the town by the train... Ha Ha.

Returning safely to the ship in the afternoon it was again a relaxing period prior to the usual evening events of drinks, followed by a very pleasant dinner in our allocated Restaurant, Luminae. And, I must say that this ship was a pleasure to be on and the food and service were excellent.

The next day was pretty much a non-event, with the ship docking at, Icy Strait Point.

This was basically the landing site for the "city" of Hoonah.

I don't know why it is referred to as a city, as the few shops at the berth terminal appeared to have more retail outlets than Hoonah.

This region is noted for its' local native population, The Tlingit Indians and a number of timber buildings in the town were built by them. The only plus this day for us, was the reasonably close sighting of a huge Eagle and her siblings, nesting in a tree just to the side of the main through road of the "city".

The older bird taking flight at one point and showing off her massive wingspan, which must have been at least six feet across. This sighting was worth the 5 dollar each return Shuttle Bus ride to Hoonah, a short distance from the port.

The day following we were scheduled to do a day trip in the rather larger township of Ketchikan. This name reminds me of mail we have received over the years, especially prior to email, when for some reason, our correspondents would spell Kenchington incorrectly.

We had the often-spelt error... Ketchinham, but our favourite has always been the one envelope addressed to: Mr. Ken Ching Tong! They must have thought I was Chinese.

Well in Ketchikan this day a much larger retail area was evident, the shops are still very much the same; Jewellers, gift shops and crab shacks. I'm not sure where the locals go for their supplies, apparently transported to this region by water, at a higher expense to the locals, with no road or rail connection due to the vast wilderness surrounds and the impassable mountains.

These never-ending Jewellery and gift shops must surely be of little use to the locals. We did however spot one man carrying shopping bags from his car to his unit with, "Safeways" emblazoned on the side of one bag, so this supermarket was presumably situated on the town's outer region.

Our particular day trip, 10.30am to 3.00pm, commenced with a half hour coach ride to a small private harbour. Here we then switched to a diesel- powered passenger boat, seating about twenty, taking us all out across the huge sea lake to view eagles nesting along the foreshore.

These birds are so large that you could easily mistake them for a small plane, once they are in the high of the sky.

Crossing this very large lake we also had the occasional whale tail sighting. There were also large fish observed along the way and a little while before our trip was complete, we stopped and pulled onto the boat a large crab pot. Several crabs were contained inside it and our tour guide explained how these crabs are caught and which can be taken. Six inches across their back shell being the minimum size and other, smaller ones are returned to the ocean bed. Completing the discussion with various passengers handling the biggest crustacean, we headed back to our port for a very anticipated lunch of several, large crab legs and beer. The

Ketchikan Centre Monument of Early Miners.

Arial View of Ketchikan

restaurant room itself faced the lake, with boating activity aplenty being observed.

It was a busy area altogether and obviously not just for the tourists. The service staff were very competent and the service was excellent and crabs and beer just kept 'flowing'.

Our companions eating so many crab legs it was embarrassing to watch, although the crabs were… scrumptious!

The following day was the last day at sea and our on-ward journey to Vancouver. That afternoon we entered Canadian waters and the Inside Passage, which for the next few hours provided spectacular scenic views and the occasional glimpse of wildlife.

Vancouver here we come!

VANCOUVER

We arrived in Vancouver port around 7.00 am and were already showered and dressed, with our small bags packed and ready to go. Our large suitcases already dispatched the evening before, having placed these outside our cabin for collection by the crew, to be delivered to the downstairs storage/dispatch section.

Following a good breakfast we joined the queues, waiting our allotted time to disembark the ship. Getting off, we walked along the enclosed port building, stopped only briefly to pick up our awaiting main luggage and then it was off into the Customs area. Stopped even more briefly by two local Border Force Officers, enquiring how long our stay in Canada was for and then it was out into the daylight and fresh air.

We were lucky with our hotel, The Fairmont Waterfront, as this was literally just two minutes-walk away, allowing us to wheel our luggage across the road, no taxis required!

The hotel, in fact all of the Canadian Fairmont Hotels, are now owned and managed by the French organization of Accor, a brand well known to us and certainly an expanding company in our country as well. Sofitel Hotels being one of their top brands.

The hotel was good and the main eatery, The Arc, was quite acceptable for most evening dining. However, the last evening of our stay here we planned to have our dinner out. The following day we were to relocate over to the Four Seasons Hotel, this being, “the tour hotel”, organised by Tauck, as the first accommodation part of our ten-day tour.

Our dinner out was taken at the other Fairmont Hotel, The Pacific Rim, a short walk away and the hotel that the Prime Minister, Mr. Trudeau was staying at, being in Vancouver at the same time as us. We did see him in his chauffeur driven Limo one day, with a number of police on motorbikes escorting him, but that was our only sighting.

Anyway, this hotel’s newly refurbished restaurant, The Botanist, was excellent.

First class meals, served by very competent staff and after dining we walked over to the open kitchen, facing the restaurant and introduced ourselves and shook hands with the head chef, Hector. He told us he was originally from Mexico, and we had a very friendly chat and thanked him and his staff for our excellent dinner.

He seemed a little surprised by our approach … a customer coming over to thank him personally… he obviously doesn't know many Australians!

Vancouver is an easy city to explore and we quickly found our way to the shopping malls and quality boutiques (not that we bought much at all) and of course we also identified a couple of good coffee shops providing decent espresso coffee!

The city is very safe and clean, but there is a major problem with homeless people in most sectors of the city, some even sleeping in the main street areas and apparently police have a limited legal avenue to move them on. A two-week period of notice to 'relocate' was apparently a legal requirement, suggested to us by a local!

Certain areas were worse than others, sometimes you were asked for money, but mostly they kept to themselves, but even so this negativity is confronting.

Some city locations we avoided returning to, after witnessing these issues.

One disappointment we did have was China Town. A magazine placed in our hotel room which we read, exuded the wonders of this area and made it sound wonderful. However, on visiting this rather large section of Vancouver, approximately a twenty-five-minute walk to the east of our hotel, it bore very little resemblance to what was written in that magazine. It was quite apparent that this magazine article was either written some years before or was written from memory! Many shops were shut down, many shops were vacant, displaying, "For Lease" signs and most of the shops that were open, had dirty shop fronts. There were extremely poor displays in those that were open and the featured Chinese Botanic Garden was overgrown with weeds and filthy. All a complete disgrace in our minds and certainly not worthy of that magazine article!

Our Fairmont hotel was right at the front of town virtually fronting the main, Coal Harbour Marina, with many ships docking over our five-day stay here. Virtually all following a similar line as us, from Anchorage down through the same Alaskan ports, before the Vancouver finish.

From this location we would often walk along the waterfront and into the adjoining park, which was terrific and of course, still right in the city's sector.

Our next hotel that we were moving to the following day, was not too far away and was the selected hotel by Tauck Tours for the commencement of their two back-to- back coach tours across Canada, consisting of ten days each, twenty in total, which we were looking forward to.

Coal Harbour Marina

Cruising the Inside Passage, through to our stop in Vancouver.

The Tauck Tour

The following day, Wednesday, we relocated to the Four Seasons Hotel, a short taxi ride away. We could have walked, but I didn't think dragging our suitcases down the busy main street was a good idea.

This day was actually a day earlier than the official tour commencement, but we wanted to adjust to our upcoming event, officially commencing the next day, Thursday.

I must say that we were pleased that we did not book into this hotel initially, as it was not as good as the Fairmont (although a similar price structure) and the dinner, we had that evening in the hotel's restaurant was not brilliant!

The following day we were expected to meet with all of our fellow travellers and our Tauck Tour guide at 6.00pm that evening

We had already viewed a fair amount of Vancouver city by this time so most of this day was relaxing in and around the hotel and its' immediate surrounds. At the allotted time, of 6.00pm, we ventured down to our meeting point. Following a short gathering and a few brief introductions, we were all ushered into a private dining room for a very pleasant dinner organised by Tauck.

This dinner was certainly better than the previous evening's disappointment.

Our Tour Guide, or Tour Director to give him his correct title, was Greg Dickie, a long time Tauck Guide and a relative local to that region. His instructive guide and obvious local knowledge made for a very informative trip and a very good one at that.

Although he was a resident of this region, he had utilised his tour guide skills across a few other countries as well and certainly his time with us was well structured and his manner was excellent, with a little humour thrown in!

Day 1

This was mostly consisting of getting to the hotel, nominated by Tauck and the dinner as previously mentioned and was designed, no doubt to have everyone get to our allotted hotel on time. Well, all the travellers appeared to have settled into The Four Seasons and settled into the feel of our surroundings and the city. This initial get together was relaxed and Greg outlined his way of "guiding" to us and set out his programme for the next 9 days.

Meeting all our fellow travellers was interesting, with nearly all being Americans, with one couple from New Zealand and fairly all being of a similar age group and mostly retired like us.

Day 2

Well, this day was the main commencement of our tour and following breakfast and all of the large luggage placed onto our coach, it was off to our first 'port' of call. Stanley Park and an Art Gallery, were our first destinations, followed by lunch at the Granville Market.

Stanley Park is on a peninsula, with surrounding ocean and covers an area of some 1000 acres, with many Cedar trees, Fir Trees and as confirmed by Greg our tour guide, "ever blooming gardens"!

There are many walking paths and I think I lost a kilo or two here with the walking my wife made me do!

Onto Granville Market and this is mostly a huge fresh food market, providing Seafood, Meats, Cheeses and Dairy products and has a large Food Court, where lunch was taken, in a smaller cafe section.

This day was a jammed packed day and following our leisurely lunch, we were back on the coach and heading down to a particular section of the port area. Here we would be jumping on a Flying Boat, or "Floatplane" as it was described and taking a 30-minute flight over to Victoria on Vancouver Island.

Now I'm not a very good passenger on a plane at the best of times and my preference is to fly on the largest plane there is so, a small flying boat…Mmmm!

There were 3 "Floatplanes"* altogether, to accommodate the approximately 40 of us. This area in the bay was quite full with this type of aircraft and obviously a fairly well used method in this region to move both people and products around.

It was an interesting experience, but inside the plane it is very noisy, with the engines of these planes, reasonably, up close and personal! Not much conversation going on, just the odd smile and nod to your fellow traveller.

Thankfully there were no mishaps, the water landing fairly smooth and we arrived safely at our 'berth' on a marina sector of the island. Re-assembling on the dock side, we then headed for our same coach (it having driven over via a ferry connection). It was then off to our allotted hotel, The Hotel Grand Pacific, for a 2-night stay.

It would also appear, that a number of these planes have been involved in crashes, over the past few years!

* About 18 months after our "Floatplane" trip, we heard on the news of a mid-air collision of 2 of these aircraft in that same region. A few people were killed.

Day 3

The hotel was good and we enjoyed a dinner with our, new 'travel-mates' and got to talk with a few of them, including the couple from N.Z., who were from the South Island and enjoying their first visit to Canada, like us.

Following a quite relaxed buffet style breakfast the next morning, we all boarded our coach for a short sightseeing morning of the Butchart Gardens, which included a snack lunch. These Gardens are classified as a National Historic site and cover an area of around 55 acres of gardens, with apparently over 900 varieties of plants.

Leaving the gardens, we were back on the coach and onto Victoria, to the Empress Hotel for … High Tea!

Following this we were, 'set free', to explore on our own and if required, free tickets were issued to visit the Royal British Columbia Museum.

A section of The Butchart Gardens.

We decided to just have a tourist's day and wander through the shopping zone and mix with the locals and see how they lived. We also enjoyed a coffee and cake that afternoon and then it was back to the Grand Pacific hotel in time for an early dinner on our own.

Day 4

Once again, an early breakfast this day, as we were moving on from Vancouver Island and heading back to the mainland. Relocating this time on our allotted coach and travelling via the ferry crossing. Much safer than a, 'floatplane'!

It was to be a busy day and after a quite relaxing 45-minute ferry ride back to Vancouver, situated inside the ferry, we once again boarded our coach and headed to an area of lower Vancouver called, Gastown.

My wife and I had actually been around this section of Vancouver during our previous few days stay, so knew some of its' highlights. Although, nothing much to highlight in this section of the city!

Here we had around an hour wait, eventually boarding the Rockies Train, which would take us on a most anticipated overnight train ride to Jasper.

Our large luggage bags were removed from the coach to a storage section of the train, leaving us with only our smaller bags, with notable "essentials" for our overnight journey.

We were shown to our cabin for the journey and following a safety briefing by the train staff, we were "herded" together with our fellow travellers into our very own seating area, the Panorama train car. It was here that "Bon-Voyage" champagne was awaiting! Greg, our tour director, certainly had 'style'!

Following this, we enjoyed lunch and later dinner in the dining section next to this area. However, following a pleasant lunch, we headed to a viewing platform to view the magnificent scenery of the mountains that surrounded us.

What a wonderful scene was before our eyes, the highest and whitest snow- capped mountains one minute and then low-level rock sections next, constantly changing, although still mountainous. No 'Grizzlies' were spotted in this area though.

Greg, had previously that day made the statement that, "some guests may wish to bring along their own personal refreshments to enjoy in the privacy of their own room"! He had made this trip before… obviously.

I must say that we were pleased we did have a little 'quaffer' with us, making for a much better night's sleep in that quite small bunk-bed room!

Day 5

The train journey was reasonably uneventful and much better than a similar overnight train journey we had experienced a few years earlier on the Ghan trip to Darwin.

We were up early, but no breakfast on the train, this would be taken a little later at our hotel. A quick freshen-up (no shower to be taken in the small ablutions section of our room) and then a repack of our luggage and readying ourselves for the next stage of our trip in this famous region.

We arrived early into the city of Jasper and removing ourselves and our luggage from the train, we were transported to our place of accommodation for the next two nights. "The Fairmont Jasper Park Lodge", welcomed us shortly after 8.00am, but rooms would not be available until the afternoon.

At around 9.00am we were all ushered into the restaurant and a very pleasant breakfast was served. Following this we had a brief review of our surroundings, before we prepared for our next trip that day, "A Rafting Boat trip on calm waters", we were informed!

Well, this was not a totally calm waterway, but having been provided with a full-length clear plastic body-suit we did keep the splashes at bay. And very thankful was I, when the water did

Jasper Park Lodge adjacent to the Jasper National Park Lake

flow over the side of the boat … and the seated area I was in. That plastic body-suit keeping my bum dry!!

The boat trip was only for about an hour and not overly exciting!

On our return to dry land, we were treated to a very pleasant BBQ lunch at the local Golf Course Clubhouse.

Following our lunch, it was back onto our coach for a drive into, Malign Canyon, a region of lakes and waterfalls and of course, certain bird life and apparently, the odd wild Beasty!

Well, we saw no wild hairy things, only a couple of quite large eagles, but the large lakes and the associated, Glacial fed waterfalls flowing into them, were very beautiful. It was then back on the coach and heading back to our new hotel, to officially book-in at 4.00pm.

Completing the now usual, check-in, handing over our credit card details to pay for any 'extras' we may have…again read wine here, it was up to our room and get ourselves prepared for an early dinner.

After a very nice dinner it was off to a welcoming bed for a good night's sleep and looking forward to the next day, "A leisure day" …

Day 6

Ah, today is a slow "personal day", no tour schedule and our Tour Director, Greg recommends a late breakfast and a, "Slow Day" enjoying a, "day in the Rockies"!

So, following a very pleasant buffet breakfast, we ventured around the hotel grounds, sections of which included large parts of the adjacent local golf course. All very green and lush, adding to the style of this very pleasant hotel.

Yes, a very lazy day was our intention and although some laundry duties were undertaken in the hotel guests' laundry … very convenient, we did relax.

And following this it was more walking and enjoying time by ourselves.

The retail sector is not huge, with a number of stone buildings and very much an adventurist's playground, rather than a shopper!

Jasper is in the Alberta Province and noted as an, Alpine Town, with one of the largest parks in this Rockies region.

On a clear sky night, the Milky Way Galaxy of stars are so prominent and again, a recognised feature of this sector.

Dinner was also a relaxed affair and on offer were a selection of dining facilities, with 3 main eateries in the hotel. We chose the Emerald Lounge … no reservation required and a relaxed and informal environment in the Grand Lodge.

The next day would again be a travelling day and our main luggage was to be packed and ready for collection at 6.30am!

Day 7

Following a very early brekky this day and payment of our … mostly drinks bill, it was onto the coach and departing at 8.00am, heading for the very famous, Chateau Lake Louise.

On the journey this morning we would be taking a very interesting detour and would be stopping at the Athabasca Glacier at around 10.30am.

Arriving here we transferred to a, 'Snocoach', for a drive over the Glacier itself. Wow!

Once on the 'Snocoach' we set off across the snow covering the coach park we had pulled up at and then straight onto the Glacier itself. The coach actually stopping and allowing the travellers to get off and actually walk over a section of the, Athabasca Glacier … Double Wow!!

We were told to, "tread carefully", it can be quite slippery and Greg said, "he did not like the sight of blood"!

This particular Glacier is located in the Jasper National Park and is 'fed' by the Columbian Ice Fields. It has been slowly reducing over the past years and is estimated to have lowered by around 1.5 klms. In the past 125 years.

It currently reduces by approximately 5 mtrs. per year and has been suggested that, with Climate Change it could disappear in the next Generation!

Well, sunglasses were definitely required, with the very bright reflection of the glacier surface and surrounding white topped mountains. Sturdy footwear also a requirement, with the sometimes undulating and slippery ice-covered surface.

A warm jacket also being a must, although it was not as cold as we thought it might be, with a temp of around 10c.

More and more coaches were arriving and many walkers were now parading with us.

This sector of the Glacier was quite large and although more walkers were out of their coaches and stretching their legs, it didn't feel overcrowded.

After about an hour of this very different experience it was back on the 'Snocoach', returning to our normal coach back in the, by now, quite busy coach park area.

Our next stop was a very welcome lunch at the Saskatchewan River Crossing, in a quite relaxed surrounding. This region is located in the Banff National Park, in Western Alberta.

Following lunch, it was back onto our coach and off on a couple of hours drive to the world famous, Lake Louise and that CHATEAU!

Another big … WOW! … No better place to stay when in this region!

Pictures of this Lake and Chateau are of course numerous, but it's not until you actually stand at the Lake front and view this scene for yourself, that you can fully appreciate the all-encompassing power of being there.

Well, it was to be only one night here, with another relaxing dinner, at any of the five venues on site, from casual eating, to a more formal dinner. As we were only here, at this quite special location for one night, we decided on booking into the Fairview Restaurant for an, "Elegant Fine Dining" experience.

Yes, we did get a little dressed up for this evening and enjoyed a very good dinner, sat next to a window, overlooking the wide Lake with that, 'million-dollar' view.

After a relaxing, 'night-cap', it was up to our room and once again preparing our luggage for a morning pickup. Although a later time was scheduled to have all the bags ready, as we were to have a group photo by the Lake and we did not have to join the

The Fairmont Lake Louise Hotel AND… the very famous Lake Louise.

Coach until 11.45am. We would then be off to the final destination of this ten-day tour, a two day stop in the city of Banff and our hotel, the Banff Springs Hotel.

Day 8

Once again, back on the coach, but a late start today with a group photo taken, showing a very happy bunch of travellers. With this late start, lunch was a little later and taken on our journey at a small roadside style of café and was simple, but good.

We arrived at the Banff Springs Hotel around 4.00pm and what a magnificent looking hotel it is.

After booking in, my wife and I headed out to the main city area, to check out the "local scene".

There was a quite large shopping section, with an Arcade containing a food hall and a, 'Canadian Ski Museum' and so a

good walk was taken, to balance out the time spent, too much time spent...sitting in a coach!

However, our walk was a little limited as time was marching on and so we headed back to the hotel to prepare for our up-coming dinner. A dinner which was unremarkable and no doubt associated to being a little tired from the day's travel. Bedtime was calling!

Day 9

Our day starts slowly with a late breakfast, followed by an early 'morning coffee'. Once again, today is a "Leisure Day" and we are free to spend time doing, "whatever takes our fancy", according to Greg. So, it's off out to downtown Banff, where the Museums are supposed to be and also as directed by Greg, "The places to go"! However, we are more inclined to visit the shopping areas and check out the local region and maybe chat to a local or two.

After a couple of hours of good walking we are of the view that the town is quite similar to most that we have already visited, so

The Fairmont Banff Hotel

we decide to head back to our hotel and relax, prior to preparing for dinner.

This will be our last dinner on this sector of this tour and will include a, “Farewell Reception” of a few drinks and nibbles, prior to Greg’s organised dinner in the hotel’s restaurant.

Tomorrow we are scheduled to have an early breakfast at 6.30 am, with our bags all packed and ready for collection, as we will be leaving the hotel at 8.00am for the Calgary Airport, a two-hour drive away.

From here we will all be going our separate ways, with this section of our tour completing.

Most of our fellow travellers, being American, will be heading home to their particular cities. We on the other hand will be joining a flight to Toronto for our next section of our Tauck Tour. Another 10 days, this time heading east across the country, visiting the major cities on this eastern side of Canada. This sector will also include a stop that we are very much looking forward to, Niagara Falls.

Our farewell drinkies session is very relaxed and after a couple of speeches, from both Greg and an un-rehearsed 'Thank-You', from one of our fellow travellers to Greg (which we all endorsed), it was down to an enjoyable dinner in the, Vermillion Restaurant…Tomorrow was going to be a busy day and we were looking forward to arriving into Toronto, for the start of the next ten-day tour with Tauck.

Day 10

Well, here we are, the final day of our first Tauck Tour and we're up early and with bags packed, ready for collection, we head down for an early brekky at the Vermillion dining room. Saying a few "goodbyes" we head off to the coach and very soon we're on our

Times Garden, Banff National Park

way to the Calgary Airport and following an uneventful journey, we arrive on time around 10.00am.

After re-gaining our luggage we head off to our particular gate, for the usual booking in and it's not long before we are boarding our plane and up, up and away, heading to the Capital, Toronto.

The flight is quite a long one, with Air Canada, taking around four plus hours, arriving at 3.15pm.

Catching a cab we head for our hotel, The Fairmont Royal York. We're booked in here for two nights and although today is officially the end of our ten-day tour, it's also Day 1 of the next tour!

The Next 10 Day Tour of Canadian Cities with Tauck

Arriving into the hotel after our reasonably long flight, was quite easy.

Canada is a large country, of some 10 million sq. klms. and you start to understand why it will take 10 days to complete our Easterly journey to visit this country's major cities.

For our first night and to meet with our new Tour Director, Mindy Sjogren and our fellow travellers, a completely new group, we are to meet in the hotel lobby and then we are off to the Royal Ontario Museum for dinner.

That first evening with our initial, "Meet and Greet" was an interesting start, all gathered in the lobby, with us chatting to a number of our, new fellow travellers. With introductions complete, we boarded a coach and set off to … ROM.

A trip of close to 45 minutes and we were entering the Museum and heading for a, 'Sparkling Reception'. Yes, the Champagne and nibbles were out again and a chance to continue our chats to our fellow travellers, all joining us for this next stage of our tour.

Following this relaxed reception and enjoying a welcome relaxing champagne, we were off on a guided tour of the museum. ROM is the largest museum in Canada and certainly a stunning building, with a most modern, angled building structure adjoining the original old stone building. As with many of these public places, security is tight, with many varying displays of expensive art, sculptors and items of historical importance.

Thankfully after about an hour on tour, we were seated in the main dining area for a very welcome dinner … tiredness definitely setting in after a day's journey on planes and public transport.

Arriving back to our hotel a couple of hours later, it was up to our room and straight to bed as we were on a very special trip the next day, Niagara Falls!

Breakfast at 7.00am with the usual, bacon and eggs and a fresh orange juice (very healthy) and then onto our coach at 8.00am for a very much looking forward to, day!

A couple of hours later we are at a launching platform on the lake-side and boarding a medium sized boat called, 'The Hornblower'. This will take us on a journey across this waterway for around an hour and past the vast sector of the Falls and yes, we were told that we might get a little wet! Thank goodness for the light plastic head-to-toe 'anoraks' that were provided upon our journey's start. I know how good these outfits are!

We reached the Falls reasonably quickly and, oh boy, what a magnificent sight and to see this huge section of falls, up close from the water level is something very special. And yes, we did get a little wet!

We sailed around this sector for about twenty minutes or so, which was sufficient time and then we were off across the lake and on to the port city of Niagara-on-the-lake … Oh Gosh!!!

Whilst the Falls are something to admire, the city is not. It has a reasonably large retail sector, but appears to be just full of casinos/ gambling and gaming houses. This was not expected and was a complete eye opener, with so many casinos etc. in such a renowned region of waterways… Not attractive at all.

Following a short walk along the main shopping centre, we headed for lunch at one of the many eateries, mostly of the "fast food" style!

Following an unremarkable lunch at a burger joint and a brief walk around the main shopping precinct, it was back to join our fellow travellers. So, onto the Hornblower for a trip back to re-join our coach and then it was onto the hotel in Toronto.

A pleasant dinner was most anticipated and did not disappoint, (cost included in our Tour price… except wine!). So, we lashed out and had a Californian Shiraz from a wine region north of San Francisco, which we had actually been to on our last visit to this particular wine region. San Fran is one place we have been to a few times over the years and we look forward to travelling there again, after this virus has gone!

Finishing our dinner with a very pleasant Cognac and having had a very long day, it was off to bed, as tomorrow we are off to Ottawa, the Nation's Capital.

We were looking forward to our next stop, Ottawa, as we had arranged to catch up with friends who live here. A lovely couple who we met on a cruise some years before, Jan & Marie.

We'd called a little while before to say that we would be in Ottawa for a couple of days and arrangements were made to spend a day with them. That is one thing that may happen on your cruising journeys. Spending a couple of weeks or more on a cruise, you can meet people who you will 'click' with and enjoy time together. To catch up with friends in their backyard, especially from other countries, can be very special.

Well, it was a long and fairly full day on our journey to Ottawa. Breakfast at 7.00am and onto the coach at 8.30am and off we go, heading first to the, Big Apple in Cobourg, for a welcome coffee. It was then onto a boat (yes, another boat) and a cruise in the region called, The Thousand Islands.

This is a very large section of apparently 1800 plus islands, in the St Laurence River, which straddles the border with the U.S.A.

In this sector there are also a number of distinguished buildings, which quite often sit on the very edge of the islands in the "river/lake".

Finishing the cruise, which was interesting, with so many islands and of course, a number of Eagles in flight, we headed back to the dock.

Here we were to have lunch and alighted from the boat and took lunch right there on the harbour-side, in a quite large open shed style of eatery.

Lunch was, as anticipated in this region, a feast of very large crabs… yum-yum, oh, and a couple of beers!

Some of our travelling companions just kept on eating these tasty creatures, as the wait staff just kept on parading them around the tables on their trays. Lunch just seemed to be endless... I think we've done this before!

At 3.30 pm it was back onto the coach and departing the Thousand Islands, noted for its' very famous sauce … and very tasty with crabs!

After another long coach journey, we arrived at our hotel, The Chateau Laurie at around 5.30pm, our home for the next two nights.

An early dinner was on the cards, to be taken in the hotel's restaurant, 'Wilfred's Dining Room'. After a very busy day and travel by coach we were looking forward to this and best of all, this evening's dinner was included in our tour and again, "free"!

And tomorrow we were going to spend the day with our friends, Jan & Marie, who we had arranged to meet at the hotel entrance at a respectable, 9.00am.

Breakfast the next day was good and following a quick walk around the hotel grounds, we prepared for our day, very much looking forward to seeing our friends.

Heart Island in the St. Lawrence River.

A welcome hug and the usual greetings and … checking for the extra grey hairs and wrinkles, we climbed aboard Jan's very comfortable Honda SUV and headed off for a wonderful day's outing.

Jan & Marie were originally from Czechoslovakia and in 1968, when this country was 'invaded' by the Soviets, with their heavily armed soldiers and large tanks, to quell the, mostly student 'uprising', Jan & Marie made the decision, that it was time to leave their home country. They became eligible to emigrate to Canada and made their home in Ottawa. A great decision, I'm sure.

We were lucky to be in 'town' during the period of a magnificent local garden display at the, Jacques-Cartier Park. In this very large green sector of the city, a wonderful creation of "sculptured hedges and floral figurines", of birds, animals and humans had been established. It was such a huge selection of gardening talent that we were in awe of and the couple of hours we spent in the gardens was probably not enough, but lunch was calling!

Following lunch, we spent a wonderful couple of hours with Jan & Marie, being shown some of the region of their part of Ottawa and then we returned to our hotel, to prepare for dinner.

Ottawa is certainly a city I would very much like to visit again and seeking out the Parliament building and the historical and canal region would be a highlight.

For dinner, Jan and Marie had chosen a favourite of theirs, Giovani's Italian Restaurant, where we had an excellent dinner. This rounded off a terrific day spent with our, "shipmate friends" from a cruise of some years' before.

We very much look forward to reciprocating when Jan and Marie enable a "bucket list" holiday in Australia, when life gets back to some sort of normal, following Covid.

The following day it was another travel day, with us on the coach and heading for Montreal.

The Sculptured Displays at the Jacques-Cartier Park were Excellent.

Day 5

It was to be another long coach journey, leaving at around 8.30am, with lunch taken early at about midday in a hotel called, Chateau Vaudreuil. This hotel was of the usual 'look', of red brick exterior and pale green roof. It was situated along-side a lake and the surrounding grounds were well manicured. A similar variety of shrubs and plants as viewed in many other similar grounds were very much in evidence.

The lunch was very good, taken in one of what looked like, a number of dining areas spread across the building. We finally arrived at our next 2-night stop at the Fairmont Queen Elizabeth Hotel in Montreal, at around 4.30pm.

Montreal is in the Quebec Province and therefore you are hearing a little more French spoken and seeing signs in both French and English.

The hotel is very good, with most of the building being of an older historical stone and brick structure.

For us, Montreal was not the most inspiring of cities and our coach did take us on a brief tour of the city, whilst heading for our hotel. Although in addition to this, a walking tour had been organised with other members of our Tauck tour and was interesting and our completion of this walking tour was down at the old port sector, which was a visual attraction and of the most interest.

Day 6

Following a group photo outside the hotel in the morning after breakfast, we once again jumped onto our coach and were off for a short tour of the district and finishing once again at the port. We returned back to our hotel for lunch and a quiet afternoon, preparing for a dinner out with the group at the Bonaparte Hotel restaurant in old Montreal.

This was situated in the older part of Montreal, in a section of mostly retail shops and dinner was a little more French, as you would imagine, with a name like, Bonaparte!

Day 7, 8 & 9

Quebec City… Well, Once again having an early breakfast, bags packed and at 8.30am we're jumping back on to the coach, with all our traveling companions and luggage. We're off to the city of Quebec and our next three days we will be bedding down at the, Fairmont Le Chateau Frontenac. (All in separate rooms of course!).

On our journey to the Chateau, we stop for a sightseeing walk and Gondola ride at the, Montmorency Falls, before we have lunch here.

The Chateau Frontenac (shown below), is a magnificent elevated hotel with great views over the St Laurence River. It was built by the Canadian Railway Company in the late 19th Century, together with other Chateau Hotels, to encourage travel through this region. It is a stupendous looking complex, with high towers

GEOMANIA

Sections of the old town retail outlets of the, Quartier Petit Champlain, Quebec City.

and "pointy rooves", with the Montmorency National Park and city stretching out below, just a few minutes-walk away. You would not want to stay in any other place!

Quebec City, being a very French dominated sector of Canada is, if I might say, different. Many of the locals appear to be a little more, 'stiff', in both their speech with you and their approach. However, we found the shops and surrounding public areas to be very clean and welcoming in the main.

Being in Quebec City for two full days (3 nights), allows us to spend a fair amount of time by ourselves, walking the city area, looking at a few markets and generally window shopping…of course!

The old town of Quebec, with many historic buildings, some dating back to the 17th century, is a wonderful region to visit, with a few cobblestone pathways, between many 'good looking' retail sections.

A couple of tours were organised by Tauck, which included a visit to, Ile d'Orleans, a charming little island in the St Laurence River, which is noted for the production of several fruit and vegetable items, including apples.

Here we had a pleasant lunch and this was followed by an enjoyable tasting of a few local Ciders. Hic!

Finalising our 9-day tour, of course, was a 'Farewell Dinner', with the usual Champagne and nibbles reception at the start, followed by a fine dinner in the Chateau's best restaurant.

The Chateau Frontenac hotel was a wonderful place to complete our Canadian tour and certainly is one stop that we hope to get back to in the future.

The following day of, 'moving house', was its' usual start of packing bags, paying our drinks bill and then, no coach this time, we're catching a local taxi to the airport. We are flying off to a location we have been to a few times before, San Francisco. Here we are booked in for a couple days at our favourite hotel here, The Ritz Carlton. This hotel is located up on one of San Fran's famous hills, 'Nob Hill', with the city itself a pleasant walk away… and we'll also be back there one day!!

This visit though was only for two nights, so following our plane journey across from Quebec and checking into the hotel after lunch, we were mostly restricted to one day of being a tourist.

Having been in this city before we knew what we would do, following a pleasant and relaxed breakfast…A relaxing walk down to the marina area and Fisherman's Wharf and view the Seals on the rocks, yes Seals. Following this and our usual "window shopping", it's a lunch at a waterfront restaurant.

The other significant visual aspect here is looking across to the historical island of, Alcatraz. Once a major prison, but not anymore and now a tourist attraction, which my wife and I did visit (with a tour guide) on a visit a few years ago… interesting but once is enough!

Yes, San Francisco is a great city to visit and one where I must say we have always felt safe in.

San Francisco City, fronting San Francisco Bay and the "very special Island" on the following page, although no in-mates these days, with the Golden Gate Bridge behind.

We're Wining and Dining ... Our Last Travel Before Covid-19 Appears.

Well, here we are in Singapore, having flown in with Singapore Airlines, arriving late afternoon in late September 2019. This is our first flight on Singapore Airlines for some time, having utilised Emirates Airlines for quite a while, preferring to pass through Dubai and spend a few days there.

We are booked into the, "So-Sofitel Hotel", yes, that is the name, a new hotel experience for us.

We're here for 3 nights, prior to flying on to London, Heathrow and set to enjoy a short holiday in U.K. of around two weeks. Here we'll be catching up with family and friends, before our escape on the cruise ship, Oceania Nautica and a 12-day cruise along the French coast and then on to Portugal and then Spain, completing our cruise in Barcelona.

Singapore has grown considerably over the years and significantly in the roughly ten-year period since we were here last.

Still a great place to visit, although the very clean and 'calm' environment that was here on several visits we have previously made over the years, is not so evident. This time we note several shortcomings in "tidiness" that would not have been tolerated in years gone by. Things like cigarette butts on the ground and the odd empty can or empty bottle discarded into the garden beds, that would have been totally frowned upon years ago. The population is now almost six million people, this figure more than double that of our very first visit, over thirty years ago and I suppose with this level of residents in such a small area of land, it can alter the overall status quo.

Still, it's a great country to visit and the three days we are here go very quickly. Although we do manage to squeeze in a visit to the, Long Bar of the Raffles Hotel which, when we arrive in Singapore, has only just re-opened following a full refurbishment, apparently taking around a year to complete.

I must admit that a pint of Tiger Beer and a very famous, Singapore Sling cocktail, at $65 is a little over the top, but hey ... this is The Raffles Hotel.

The Raffles was built in 1887, although added to and extended over the years and named after the founder of Singapore, Sir Stamford Raffles.

It is very much noted in many novels by Somerset Maugham, the English writer, who spent many years there, before moving to Paris in his later years.

We are to return to Singapore in just over a months' time for only two days, on a stopover, before returning to Brisbane in late October.

Flying out of the "Lion City" and looking out of our window, we greatly admire the very plush region of gardens that surround the Changi Airport.

This airport is one of the best in the world and over the past few years has been added to by large garden areas, both inside the terminals and outside, in the surrounding sectors. Large waterfalls and significant "greenery" and floral sections abound, making your travel wait time relax you!

We arrived at Heathrow in the late evening and once clear of Immigration and other formalities, we walk through the airport complex in the direction of the airport's Sofitel Hotel, very conveniently situated. Yes, this is "just" a Sofitel ... where we will spend only the one night prior to collecting our Avis Hire car in the morning and starting off on our much awaited catch-up with family and friends.

Collecting our 'hire car' the following morning, a Hyundai SUV....specially selected by me, believing it to have compatible controls, similar to our cars at home, didn't quite work out. Our Hyundai had the indicators and wiper stalks reversed, to meet the European standard...Duh!

So, for the next few days the windscreen was wiped clean every time I wanted to indicate a turn!

The Raffles Hotel on the top, is from a period long ago!

The Marina Bay Hotel shown here is very much the modern-day equivalent!

Merlion Park Singapore

Never mind, we got over that and the vehicle handled our, Southern England trip very well, especially given all the weighty luggage we had brought with us for our, nearly six-week stint of travel. Two large suitcases, two 'wheely' carry-ons and two large 'Duffle Bags'! Too many items and ... when will we learn what to pack?

Leaving the Avis office that day we headed out of this major region to the area of Maidenhead, not too far from Windsor, to meet up with our life-time friends, John and June who live in a lovely area, adjacent to a very large field. On the other side of this field is located the village of Bray and in this, reasonably large village there are a couple of very fine, famous restaurants, including perhaps the most famous, Heston Blumental's, "The Fat Duck".

We are staying two days with John & June, with John's old school mate and our friend Richard flying in from the U.S. (where he now lives), joining us for one day, prior to heading north to Scarborough to visit his Mum, who had recently turned 90. Needless to say, that the day we all spent together consisted mostly of eating, drinking and talking. And, all of this prior to visiting a couple of terrific restaurants, for lunch and dinner, to continue same! This "catch-up" was nearing the 50th anniversary of my first meeting with John and Richard in 1970, when us three guys worked together in the, Saunton Sands Hotel in North Devon.

Following our London stop (and a great couple of days), we travelled south to our base in Mudeford (near Bournemouth) staying at the Harbour Hotel (previously known as the Avonmouth). We have stayed a few times at this hotel in prior years and it sits in a wonderful region of the coast. The name of Avonmouth comes from the fact that this hotel is situated virtually on the river Avon, near the township of Christchurch, again quite a pleasant region, with a few good coffee shops and restaurants.

Being in this region means we are fairly central to my England based family, both children, grand kids and my brother and two sisters.

We will be catching up with all at various times before heading to North Devon and the Saunton Sands Hotel for a few days, catching up with friends, David and Penny, who are joining us for a couple of days relaxation following the 'big' wedding of their daughter, Becky, a few days before.

Saunton Sands Hotel is a wonderful hotel, virtually right on the beach, where myself, John and Richard came to work a 'Summer Season', of around six months.

We were all waiters in the hotel's restaurant and completing our time there (at the winter closure), we set off on a unique and a first for all of us, our first European holiday.

Driving down through France and then Spain and on down to the coastal town of Benidorm, spending about a month there. Returning home, a couple of months later I continued on for a couple of years at the hotel, from Christmas 1970 till October '73, completing 3 Seasons in total.

It was at this point that I started my long management career in food services. ... Read my book, "I was going to be a Chef"!

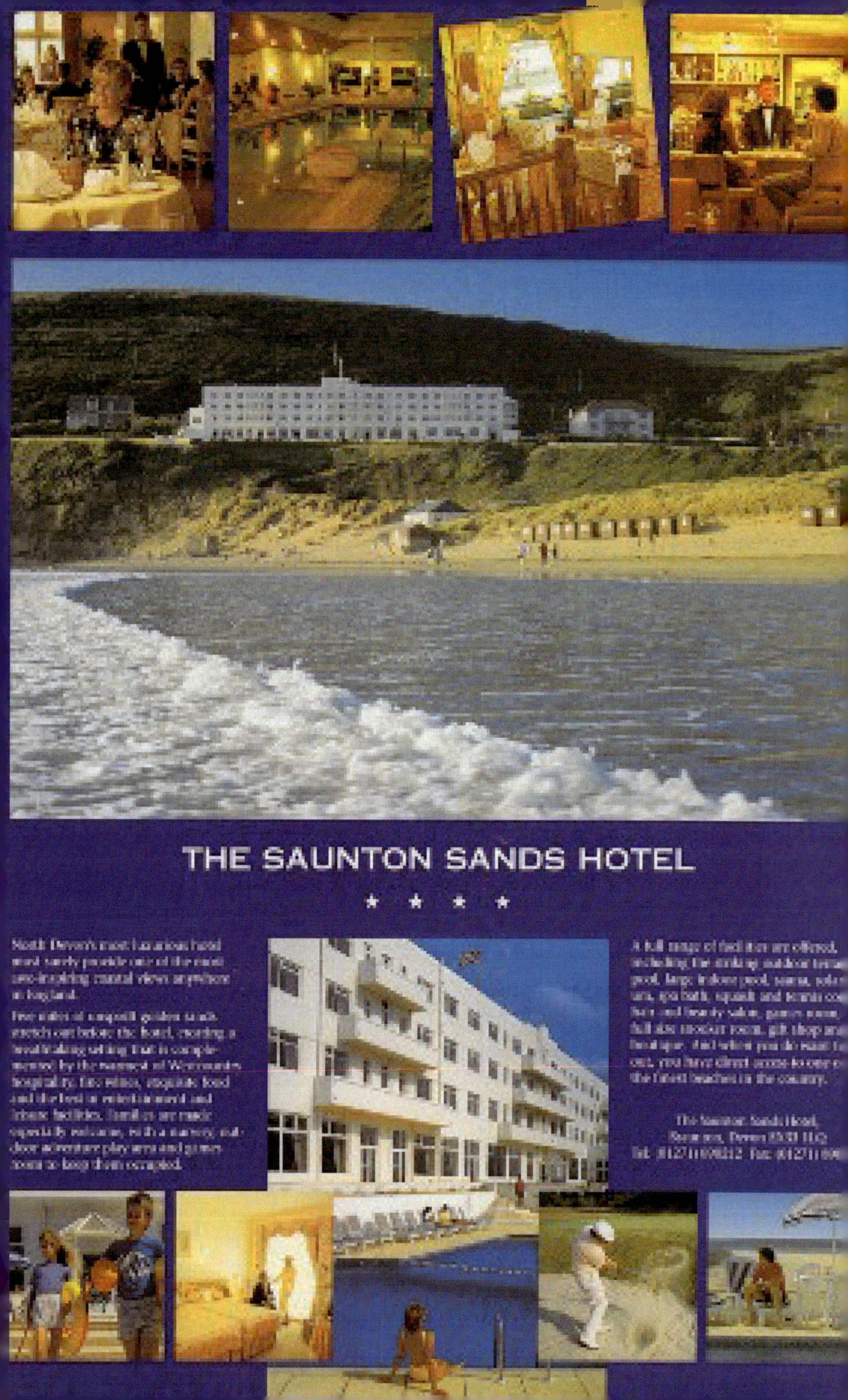
THE SAUNTON SANDS HOTEL
★ ★ ★ ★
North Devon's most luxurious hotel must surely provide one of the most awe-inspiring coastal views anywhere in England.
Five miles of unspoilt golden sands stretch out before the hotel, creating a breathtaking setting that is complemented by the warmest of Westcountry hospitality, fine wines, exquisite food and the best in entertainment and leisure facilities. Families are made especially welcome, with a nursery, outdoor adventure play area and games room to keep them occupied.
A full range of facilities are offered, including the striking outdoor terrace pool, large indoor pool, sauna, solarium, spa bath, squash and tennis courts, hair and beauty salon, games room, full size snooker room, gift shop and boutique. And when you do want to go out, you have direct access to one of the finest beaches in the country.
The Saunton Sands Hotel,
Saunton, Devon EX33 1LQ
Tel: 01271 890212 Fax: 01271 89

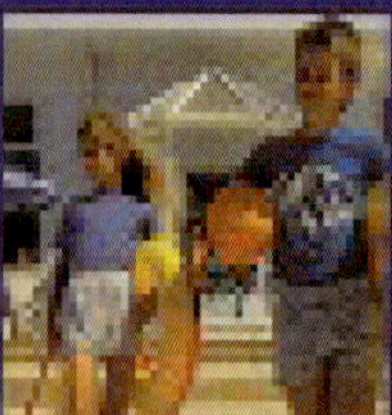

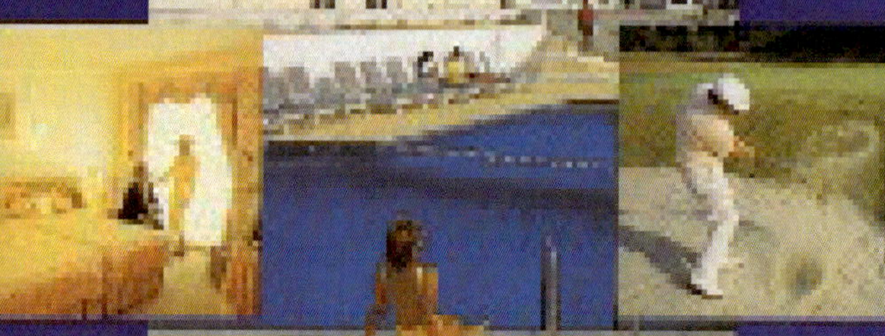

When visiting England at any time over the past years, I enjoy visiting the hotel to catch up with any of the old crew remaining in the local region, although now all have moved on, like myself. The hotel itself is still a wonderful place to spend a few days relaxing.

Having a great couple of days here with David and Penny, showing them around this wonderful coastal region, which they had not been to before. The hotel fronts a very pleasant beach, which stretches almost 5 miles in length and of course, a long walk was taken here, although a little colder than in the summer months!

Following this very relaxed two-day period, we said goodbye to David & Penny and headed back to Mudeford for a few more days catching up with family before leaving England on a pre-planned cruise, from Southampton to Barcelona on the Oceania Nautica.

Back in the south, we caught up separately with children, (not so young these days) and my siblings, celebrating my brother's birthday and enjoying family time with all and once again, "encouraging" them to visit us Downunder more often. And, of course, the grand kids are also not so young anymore and conversations with them are now a little more in-depth than on previous visits!

Following our wonderful get togethers, with all the various family members we return to our Mudeford hotel, continuing our couple of days relaxation, prior to our up- coming cruise.

This region is close to Bournemouth and as a youngster I lived about an hour bus trip away from this great city region and would often visit, to either be on the beach with mates or to the Ice-Skating rink (sat on the ice more often than not), or just to shop.

I must say though, that our visit this time to Bournemouth itself is not that good. The city's shopping sectors are now quite poorly presented and it reminds me of a "third world" country, with shop fronts looking dismal, some un-painted for several years by the look of them and some just closed down. And the famous "Bournemouth Gardens", once an attractive, large walking area from the retail sections, down to the extensive beach, is looking sad and a little abandoned by the local council. Very disappointing.

Now For That Cruise!

Leaving Mudeford and the Harbour Hotel, which is a great place to stay, with friendly staff and good eating, we head for the Port town of Southampton, around 60 minutes-drive away. This is a pleasant drive, passing through a section of the New Forest, a place I know very well, having been born and brought up on the river Avon side of the Forest, in the town of Fordingbridge.

Thankfully on this drive to Southampton we will not have the ponies skipping across the road, as they do in the central section of the Forest as this is an, "A" major road and totally fenced!

Returning our Avis hire car to their depot at Southampton Airport, we catch a taxi across to the port, arriving around twenty minutes later.

Completing the usual paperwork and security checks, we board the ship in anticipation of a great voyage, as we will be calling into a couple of great ports along the way that we have not visited before.

One of these is Bordeaux, where we have a pre-booked half-day trip out to the region of St. Emilion, with its' wonderful very old town, about 25 minutes from the centre of Bordeaux. As most will know, this is a rather huge region of vineyards, with apparently close to a quarter of a million acres under grape cultivation, with their very famous wines, known worldwide.

Boarding our ship in Southampton that morning and entering our allocated suite, I do my usual quick review of the room. On the opposite wall to the bed is the "vanity" recess section and on inspection of this area I spy on the floor, located right at the back in the corner, a little item.

Closer inspection reveals that this little item is a pill of some sort. It is Blue, with a "V" inscribed on it ...

Could this be ... a ...Viagra pill? Personally, I would not know, but it could be. Obviously, the room cleaner missed this little blighter!

Who occupied this room before us I wonder? My eyes avoided looking at the bed!

As is often the case, several Aussies are aboard for this cruise. Wherever you go on your travels you are sure to meet other Australians, who are natural travellers ... as we are.

On this cruise there are the usual American tourists and ... apparently about forty other Nationalities ... crumpets, that is a lot of Nationalities. There are only about 650 guests on board, with around 450 staff and I would imagine that the staff would equal at least half of the nationalities!

All very pleasant and well trained... as is mostly the case on these cruising liners.

On our first day, our traveling companions appear to be a little older than we have experienced on previous cruises. But over the first couple of days, they all display a more youthful appearance and as one lady was overheard to say; "Oh I always feel younger than I am"! And I guess that is how the majority of us over sixties see ourselves ... after all, in my mind I'm still only 28…It's the red wine…keeps me young!

Well, we were supposed to have our first stop in St. Peter Port, on the Isle of Guernsey, which we were both looking forward to, having not been here before. However, the weather is too rough for the Tenders, that were to be our method of reaching the dock, so this port of call is cancelled... A shame, we might make it another time!

We then sailed onto the French city of Brest, arriving the following day.

Hmmm... should have by-past this city. To quote the young Shirley Valentine…again, 'it was boring', with a number of passengers having the same opinion.

The following day we sailed on to the French city of La Rochelle, quite a pleasant enough place, not overly stunning, but a quite historic coastal city.

It has been a centre for fishing and trade since the twelfth century and its Vieux Port (Old Harbour) and huge modern Les Minimes marina make it one of the most attractive ports in France.

La Rochelle Vieux Port.

The focus of the town is the harbour, but moving into the township behind the port you find attractive buildings mostly from the 17th and 18th centuries, offering many fish restaurants and markets, with side streets well worth seeking out.

Bordeaux was the most anticipated stop and we were to have a night stayover, enabling a couple of sight-seeing days and we certainly were not disappointed.

As previously stated, our first day involved a half-day trip out to the very Medieval city of St. Emilion.

Here you find large stone buildings, with mostly stone pathways and narrow, stone-cobbled roads and in the 'village' centre itself, cars were banned ... mostly only delivery vehicles being admitted of course. The retail outlets were ... you've guessed it ... mostly wine shops, selling virtually every local variety of wine. Various sized bottles were available, even 6 Ltr. Jeroboams. Some with quite high prices, although I noted that discounts were often

Place du Palais Bordeaux.

Saint Emillion, Aquataine.

One of a number of St. Emillion wine outlets in the old town.

provided to those canny shoppers who provided a moment of ... 'hesitation', when deciding to purchase or not.

We had a very enjoyable and educational day here, visiting many of these wine outlets and we also visited the very old, Monolithic Church, with its' large stone walls, with some parts crumbled and fallen away.

The main city region of Bordeaux was made up with many fine old buildings, dating back hundreds of years and thankfully these structures avoided being bombed in the wars. Our ship was berthed right next to this sector, in the Gironde Estuary in the Dordogne region.

At dinner that first evening we were seated right at the very rear of the ship in the on-board, Tuscano restaurant. We had magnificent views over this section of the city buildings and the wide water view to the other side ... a great position to enjoy a lovely dinner, complete with a Million Dollar view!

The following day after breakfast, it was out to roam the city itself and although a Sunday and reasonably quiet, we enjoyed a couple of hours just strolling and of course the usual, 'window shopping' along the historical streets of this wonderful section, right next to the port.

Leaving Bordeaux early the next morning, we sailed on to another anticipated port of call, being across the border into Portugal and the Capital City, Lisbon.

We were here for only the one day and we had already planned a Food Tour for later that day, to commence around 2.00pm and finishing around 4.00pm. Time enough to re-board the ship, before our sail away at about 6.00pm that evening.

We had been to Lisbon some years' before and found it an interesting city and we enjoyed exploring the shopping areas and eating in the Piazza region at outdoor eateries.

However, this stopover felt a little different with the city's presentation, with quite a lot more tourists on the streets than we experienced previously and we felt that it had lost a little of its' charm.

We walked up and through the elevated Piazza sector and once again reviewed the shopping sections and of course, enjoying a morning coffee and a little later, a small lunch in one of the many eateries, that are presented to the exploring tourist.

With our afternoon Food-Tour commencing at 2.00pm, it left us little time to explore as much as we wanted to, so this probably contributed to not seeing a lot of the city's region as we had on our previous visit.

Lisbon is said to be the oldest city of Europe, with a population of around a million residents and it produced one of the world's great navigators, Christopher Columbus.

The history of Portugal and of Lisbon is quite in-depth and hugely interesting and further reading of its' past is definitely recommended to appreciate what is represented to today's traveller.

Our Food Tour this day was booked with an external local company and not through the ship's tour operation. We have enjoyed a couple of other Foodie experiences with this particular group when we have travelled overseas and they have been excellent.

I well remember our first tour with this group, in Rome and the young lady conducting the walking tour was an Australian, who had re-located to Italy for adventure.

On that tour it was for four hours and full of stops, both at eateries and general sectors of interest in the particular part of Rome that we were in. This sector was Testaccio and presented to us as a suburban part of the city.

All the food and beverage outlets we visited were excellent, but my memory is mostly of one particular location we paused at, a local cemetery. This sector was set amidst a virtual city of Roman ruins.

At this location our tour guide told us that a senior member of the, Bulgari family was buried, with a 'vacant' plot adjacent to this for the next family member. Also, in this cemetery was buried the English poet, John Keats. The most interesting story though was of a small, stone block-built pyramid, that we viewed and was built in this cemetery many centuries ago. It was given an upgrade in the mid 1600's but it was apparently built to accommodate a notable rich local, Caius Cestius. However, the locals, who were tasked with building this pyramid, although promised to be paid once work was complete, were never paid… So, upon the actual death of this person, instead of being 'entombed' in the pyramid, the locals apparently threw his body in the local river!

This Lisbon food tour today however, was a little…different. It could quite easily have been promoted as a "drinking tour" as we started with a sparkling wine at a local restaurant, in an old historical quarter. However, this restaurant was not that attractive or had any noted historical significance from memory, it was just a, 'kick-off' point, to welcome our group. We then moved on across the Piazza to an open front bar, where we and about 8 others in our group, were provided with a very pleasant glass of… Port!

Oh, there was a little "nibble" here…of something non-memorable, but "real" food was still not forthcoming, on this … FOOD TOUR.

Following this second stop and our glass of port, we headed further across this section of the city and our next stop was at a

The Rua dos Bacalhoeiros, with some of the many eateries in the Piazza, "foodie section" of Lisbon.

The Rio Tejo, a sector of the Port of Lisbon.

rather basic looking snack bar, situated on a walking path next to a park. Here we were provided with a glass of beer and a hot pork roll. Hmmm! The look of the pork roll did not excite me and I abstained, although the beer was good.

Following this stop we turned off this pathway and headed down the road for about 500 mtrs., to our final location where a little local eatery provided a reasonably pleasant selection of Charcuterie items, all to be enjoyed with a glass… or two of red and white wine. This restaurant was the only destination on our tour that provided some REAL food on our, "Food Tour". Ah well, you can't win them all!

On exiting this last venue, which was situated on the high point of the street, we could see down to the port area and although a little dusk by now, the ship was in sight, so we wished all our fellow Foodie Friends Bon Voyage and set off down the hill towards our steel home.

Another section of the Rio Tejo Port further along the seafront.

And yes, we were looking forward to having a wonderful dinner… with food, back on board!

SEVILLE ... CADIZ SPAIN

Sailing away from Portugal we have one day at sea, relaxing and doing the usual … dining and wining and taking life easy.

Next day we are arriving at the port of Cadiz, with the main city of Seville a short bus ride away and the promoted destination of this stop.

We have been to this region once before some years prior and always wanted to return as the last time we were on a driving holiday and arriving into Seville could find no real parking areas and having got tied up in busy traffic sectors, with frustration setting in, we just left town and moved further along the coast.

So, we were looking forward to having some time exploring the Seville area in particular.

The port of Cadiz is our starting point, with our cruise ship taking its' berth around 7.00am and with all the necessary passport control and customs duties being completed, albeit limited, we are off and running.

We decide not to do any booked tour today, but catch one of the allotted shuttle buses scheduled to take all to Seville.

This city is the largest city of southern Spain and of course again, an historic centre with many fine, very old buildings, which would take a few days to visit them thoroughly and investigate their rich history. We only have limited time, so we choose to walk and just take in all that's in our path, so to speak. However, the Seville Cathedral and the sector that it is in, a lush park with

lake, is rather stunning, so a little more time spent here.

I am not a religious person, but I do admire these magnificent structures, built many hundreds of years ago and I am in wonder of the workmanship involved in the building of these massive structures all those years before, without the modern-day machinery we have at our disposal today. This cathedral was built over quite an extensive period, from the year 1400 to 1506.

It is by now early afternoon and we think a typical Spanish lunch of Paella at a small local restaurant, is the way to go. Yes, we strike it lucky and lunch is just delicious and very Spanish! Following this very enjoyable lunch stop we head across to the bus pick-up point and jump on board, heading back to Cadiz for a stroll around this port city.

Here there are many cobblestone streets and of course many old buildings.

Being at this port of call for only a one-day trip, time is obviously limited to see everything and we probably would like to see the shops and the food markets more than the historical buildings, to see how, "the other half live".

Sometimes meeting a few locals can be good fun, although language differences can be a small barrier.

Over our years of travelling, I have found that once you mention to a local that you are Australian, their reaction is always friendly and positive. Quite often they have relatives or friends

PATRIOTISMO
CADIZ A MORET

The Castle of Santa Barbara, Cadiz

Costa de la Luz, Cadiz

living in OZ and are interested in talking with you about the localities in which their relatives live.

I always find these discussions interesting and talking to locals about their region invites a knowledge that you otherwise may not get, from just looking!

On this walk we visit a rather large supermarket and check out the fruit and veg section and the butcher sections and the various price structures. This can be quite enlightening, although the sight we see in the meat section of many whole baby piglets, on display ... ready for roasting ...could cause you become a vegetarian. Following this visit to the market, we head back to the port and board our steel home for the next part of this delightful journey.

GRANADA Port of Motril

Leaving Cadiz, we sail onto the next port of Motril, passing through the Gibraltar Strait, although not much to view, being a night time sail.

We arrive into the port early morning, in readiness for an 'escape' to Granada.

However, we are informed by our ship's daily news letter that this day, a Saturday is a public holiday in Spain and therefore most places will be closed and the historical churches will undoubtedly be probably only open for Mass.

So, do we go or do we stay in the port area and relax?

We have been to Granada before, some years ago and remember the stunning views from this very old historical city reflecting the ancient Islamic culture of Spain. It is also home to a Moorish Palace, called the Alhambra.

The city sits reasonably high in the foothills of the Sierra Nevada Mountain range and is well worth a visit if you are in Spain. However, this day, due to the public holiday, we decide to stay in the port region and take a leisurely day and maybe ... do some washing! Yes, the ship's laundry, with ironing facilities is quiet, so here's our opportunity.

The port region is quite picturesque, with the quite blue Mediterranean Sea surrounding you and golden beaches to pass the time away, if so inclined.

The very blue Mediterranean Port of Motril

We do have a pleasant walk along the ocean front, passing a few fishermen, with a rod or two, but no fish in sight, just the odd boat and our big cruiser at one end.

There are a couple of bistro style eateries along the port side and lunch is taken at one of these, although not memorable!

Re-joining our steel home, we relax and do the usual, read a bit, afternoon tea and of course, prepare and amble down to the restaurant for dinner! What a life!

ALICANTE

Upping the anchor that late evening, we head out to sea, The Mediterranean Sea.

We are now heading to our 2nd last port, Alicante, with the prospects of another quiet day, as it will be Sunday when we berth and most shops and the banks are expected to be closed.

This will not be the first time that I have been to Alicante. I first came here in 1970, a teenager with my two mates mentioned earlier, John and Richard. We were on a first European holiday for us all. Camping most of the way down through France and Spain… Camping was not something I ever did again!

Arriving in that coastal sector of Spain, Costa Blanca, all those years ago, our main base was actually further along the coast by around 45 Klms., called Benidorm. A holiday town for sure, filled with many English and German holiday makers. Yes, baked beans on toast and sausages and mash, were all the rage!!

And one special moment of being in Benidorm, John met June, later to become his wife… and soon to celebrate 50 years of marriage…how fantastic is that.

In 1970, Spain was certainly opening up to tourism and the 'Brits' certainly loved to get some sun on their bodies, but eating Paella was not on the dinner list, so the English basics were the go.

Years later in 1989, my wife and I, together with her parents toured through this region and of course, Benidorm was on the list to re-visit. It was still very much the holiday haunt for the English and the golden beaches it was noted for were very much full.

There were many more, high-rise holiday apartments built along the beach areas and many more drinking outlets to accompany the renters. The best section of this holiday region is the old town, around a 15-minute walk of a few hundred metres, from the main beach. Here you will find typical white painted stone buildings and cobbled stone pathways, which are very much still an attraction, with a more calming presence.

So, Alicante was again to be a quiet day, with a few walks and sight-seeing of some of the old historical buildings, but from the outside only.

In 1851 Alicante was the first coastal city to be linked by train to the capital, Madrid and therefor becoming the capital's main seaport.

Well, once again, lunch was taken at one of the many seaside restaurants and sausages and mash was definitely not on our menu!

Returning to our steel home, we relaxed in our suite, preparing for an early dinner in the Tuscano restaurant, again giving us a full view of leaving the port and heading once more out to sea and on our way to our last and most anticipated final destination of Barcelona.

Here we would be disembarking and heading for the Gothic Quarter and our hotel called, Hotel Neri, where we're booked in for 4 nights.

BARCELONA

My wife and I have been to Barcelona four or five times over the past few years, staying an average of 4 or 5 nights each time and we love the city and of course the older historical sections of the Gothic Quarter.

The La Sagrada Familia Cathedral, is still being completed, after building commenced in 1882 and associated with the architect Antonia Gaudi. It is a stunning structure and a, 'must visit' attraction. Although Gaudi was not the original architect, he took over the project in 1883 and passing away in 1926, after being struck by a local Tram. He was buried in a crypt at the site.

Hotel Neri, a Relais & Chateaux hotel, is a new experience for us, having stayed at different hotels on our other visits here, except one hotel where we have stayed twice.

Our hotel selection this time was recommended by our long-term travel agents, with one of their team having stayed only recently. It is very central and quite close to this Gothic Quarter and is accessed via a cobblestone road, almost just a wide pathway.

This sector is quite extensive, with mostly cobblestone walkways in each direction, housing both holiday units and residential apartments as well as a number of retail outlets selling the usual products from clothes, shoes, art works and chemists. This sector runs adjacent to the Las Rambla stretch of shops and markets and just feels full of history.

Las Rambla was known as, Las Ramblas on our previous visits and apparently the slight name adjustment was to the conform with the Catalan pronunciation, which Barcelona is capital of in this Catalonian region.

Now … this Catalan region has long endeavoured to split from Spain and be independent, the residents considering themselves to be a separate state. However, the main government in Madrid has resisted all attempts from the Catalan people and its various officials to manage their own region.

Well, unknown to us before we set off on this holiday, unrest in the Barcelona city was increasing, with Catalan residents commencing demonstrations, endeavouring to continue their push for independence. We arrived to witness long streams of demonstrators parading up The Rambla, with the Spanish police the Guarda Civil, stationed along the way with their guns at the ready!

GREAT…we did not want to be involved in this! All we wanted was a few peaceful days, enjoying the city and its' wonderful history and restaurants, before heading off to Singapore, on our homeward journey.

We learnt that these demonstrations were occurring due to certain Catalan officials being placed in jail, due to their on-going push for independence.

Well, in the main we avoided the turmoil, but did see more and more demonstrations in late evening, when venturing out for a dinner. The hotel restaurant did not entice us, following a brief lunch there.

The immediate region around our hotel was just full of wonderful historical buildings and included here on these pages are just a few of these iconic structures.

Gaudi was certainly responsible for some of these.

Venturing out for dinner each day of our stay, the demonstrators in the later evening, when we were heading back to our hotel, mostly included the younger element of the locals. These locals appeared more intent on rioting and some even setting fire to cars in the streets. This was not good and put a big negative on this part of our holiday.

We were lucky that the majority of the street demonstrations were taking place in the evenings, so we were at least able to get out during the day and enjoy long walks, especially along the beachfront and visiting good eateries for lunches.

The big 'crunch' came however on the day we were due to leave. A one-day strike was planned and the city would be closed down … my organisation skills came into play.

Barceloneta Park

Carrer de Sant Pere Mes. Att.

Whilst our flight out was not 'till later in the day, we organised a taxi to pick us up at the hotel at 7.00am and take us to the airport early, thus hopefully avoiding the closedown commencement. And this became a very interesting decision…

We were up early, bags packed waiting for our taxi. However, the taxi driver arrived on foot and informed us that the road up to the hotel was blocked off and we would therefore have to wheel our cases about 500 metres down to his cab, parked in the main road.

Wheeling the large cases and carrying the smaller ones we set off down the cobblestone street. The taxi driver assisting us and apologising profusely as we rushed along, with suitcases bumping along the cobble-stone pathway.

And then we had a big surprise… as we approached the taxi, there in front of it was a large Guarda Civil wagon and about six policemen, with machine guns, yes, machine guns… stood outside of it. Hmmm…

Ramon Berenguer el Gran.

Thankfully, most of these 'gentlemen' were friendly and smiling at our plight, with taxi driver explaining to them what we were doing.

We loaded our luggage into the taxi and got in and ...off we set, no issues thank goodness. It was a slow trip to the airport, with a reasonable amount of traffic, mostly taxis, also heading there. However, we reached it in around half an hour after setting off.

At least arriving early, we had plenty of time to complete the usual booking-in process, although I think many travellers also had the same idea as us, as the airport was very busy.

Eventually getting through the usual Airport Security procedure we headed for the nominated Singapore Airlines room. Settling into this Club Room, a large coffee and a very welcome breakfast was taken, whilst reflecting upon a very unusual morning.

The 3 or 4 hours wait 'til our flight went quickly and once aboard we relaxed and enjoyed an uneventful flight into

Singapore. Staying just the two days, we have booked into, again a new hotel for us, The Hotel Kempinski and this was located in the slightly larger retail section of the city.

We had a relaxing couple of days, before catching our flight out to Brisbane and the Hotel Kempinski was very enjoyable, with friendly staff and completed a most memorable holiday, in more ways than one!

Reflecting back on this last trip, here in our 'Bunker', I long to once again, get on a plane, or join a cruise, even a local one and get travelling.

Canada would be one of the countries that would certainly be on our new Bucket List and again heading that way would certainly mean a stopover in San Francisco, spending more days in this city and its' region next time.

Also, Spain, a country of many wonderful sectors and Barcelona would not be missed! Hopefully now a little more settled.

Let us all hope that our vaccines keep being up-dated and we can continue to explore other parts of the world and ... live the dream!

I'm now off to enjoy a nice glass of red ... Cheers!

Acknowledgements

The wonderful photographs within the book were taken by my Darling Wife Christina, who also doubles as my Chief Editor!

I would also acknowledge the wonderful support and guidance provided by our long term Travel Agents, Melinda Gregor and Kristen Cahill and staff at Gregor and Lewis in Noosa.

One tour company I should also say a big thankyou to is Tauck, who provided a magnificent guided tour through Alaska and Canada.

Finally, the cruise lines' staff, who are always professional and friendly, making the journeys most enjoyable.